SpringerBriefs in Law

SpringerBriefs present concise summaries of cutting-edge research and practical applications across a wide spectrum of fields. Featuring compact volumes of 50 to 125 pages, the series covers a range of content from professional to academic. Typical topics might include:

- A timely report of state-of-the art analytical techniques
- A bridge between new research results, as published in journal articles, and a contextual literature review
- A snapshot of a hot or emerging topic
- A presentation of core concepts that students must understand in order to make independent contributions

SpringerBriefs in Law showcase emerging theory, empirical research, and practical application in Law from a global author community. SpringerBriefs are characterized by fast, global electronic dissemination, standard publishing contracts, standardized manuscript preparation and formatting guidelines, and expedited production schedules.

Abbas Poorhashemi
Editor

Artificial Intelligence and the Future of International Law

Bridging Rights, Trade, and Arbitration

Springer

Editor
Abbas Poorhashemi
Canadian Institute for International Law Expertise (CIFILE)
Toronto, ON, Canada

ISSN 2192-855X ISSN 2192-8568 (electronic)
SpringerBriefs in Law
ISBN 978-3-031-73333-8 ISBN 978-3-031-73334-5 (eBook)
https://doi.org/10.1007/978-3-031-73334-5

This Springer imprint is published by the registered company Springer Nature Switzerland AG
The registered company address is: Gewerbestrasse 11, 6330 Cham, Switzerland

Preface

Artificial intelligence (AI) is a cutting-edge technology that could have great potential and help humanity overcome the significant challenges it faces, such as diagnosis and treatment of diseases, management of environmental resources, fighting poverty, and sustainable development. They are also increasingly used by government officials to assess the character or skills of individuals, allocate resources, and make other decisions that can have severe and tangible consequences for human rights and the rule of law.

The development of AI in many different professions, services, and industries shows that it is essential for our current and future generations. AI is a technology that is increasingly integrating into people's lives. Although AI has numerous functions and assists in many parts, there are concerns about its potentially disruptive effects on some sectors, including international law. This evolution requires new regulations and standards to utilize this technology nationally[1] and internationally.[2]

As AI inevitably may replace many human jobs and activities, it arguably also deprives humanity of meaningful and effective participation in their lives.

[1] For instance, in June 2022, the Government of Canada introduced the Artificial Intelligence and Data Act (LIAD) as part of Bill C-27, the Digital Charter Implementation Act, 2022. LIAD represents an important step in the implementation of the Digital Charter, which aims to strengthen the confidence of Canadians in the digital technologies they use on a daily basis. The design, development, and use of AI systems must be safe and respect the values of Canadians. For more information: https://ised-isde.canada.ca/site/innovation-better-canada/en/artificial-intelligence-and-data-act-aida-companion-document.

[2] In this context, in November 2021, the 193 Member States of UNESCO meeting in the General Conference adopted the Recommendation on the Ethics of Artificial Intelligence, the first global normative instrument. Protecting human rights and dignity is the cornerstone of the Recommendation, based on the consolidation of fundamental principles such as transparency and fairness, without ever losing sight of the importance of human responsibility in the control of artificial intelligence systems. However, what makes the Recommendation exceptionally applicable are its many areas of strategic action, which enable policymakers to translate core values and principles into actions on, among others, data governance, environment and ecosystems, gender, education and research, and health and social well-being. For more, see: https://www.unesco.org/fr/artificial-intelligence/recommendation-ethics.

Furthermore, high-risk AI activity, which is far from benefiting society, can cause serious physical harm. In these circumstances, promoting reliable, robust, and trustworthy AI applications and establishing and implementing international regulations are crucial to balancing AI use and respect for international law, including human rights.

The main question is whether AI needs to be used to ensure fundamental ethics and the rule of law. From this perspective, ensuring that AI enhances human rights, not undermining them, is one of the critical factors we analyze in this book. Therefore, it is necessary to find the right balance between technological advancement, the protection of human rights, and the rule of law at national and international levels.

Regarding the definition of "artificial intelligence," we need an understandable and direct description of AI. In technical but simple terms, AI is "the study of the design of intelligent agents." In this context, an agent is "something that acts," such as a computer.[3] There is a detailed definition prepared by The High-Level Expert Group on AI in 2019: "[AI] *systems are software (and possibly also hardware) systems designed by humans that, given a complex goal, act in the physical or digital dimension by perceiving their environment through data acquisition, interpreting the collected structured or unstructured data, reasoning on the knowledge, or processing the information, derived from this data and deciding the best action(s) to take to achieve the given goal. AI systems can either use symbolic rules or learn a numeric model, and they can also adapt their behaviour by analyzing how the environment is affected by their previous actions.*"[4]

The emergence of artificial intelligence as a new technology offering a wide range of applications in both human rights[5] and the economy raises fundamental questions at the heart of existing international law. The main issue is balancing international law, including human rights and the innovation resulting from artificial intelligence. Do the utilizations of artificial intelligence require changes to existing international law frameworks regarding regulations and their implementations?

Integrating artificial intelligence (AI) systems represents a crucial convergence of technology and law, with far-reaching effects on legal discourse. From human rights to criminal law, trade law to arbitration, the implementation of AI has far-reaching implications in diverse areas of society. Through the pages of this book, we embark on a captivating exploration of international law, delving into its intricate landscape and shedding light on the complex interplay between AI and critical domains such as human rights, criminal law, trade law, and arbitration. By doing so, we aim to comprehensively review AI's fundamental principles and implications

[3] Russell, SJ and Norvig, P. (2016). Artificial intelligence: a modern approach. (3rd edition). Prentice Hall). pp. 2–4.

[4] EU High-Level Expert Group on AI. (2019). A definition of AI, main capabilities and scientific disciplines. EU Commission. p. 6.

[5] Poorhashemi, Abbas. "Principles of International Environmental Law." CIFILE Journal of International Law 4, no. 7 (2023): 80–106.

within international law. In this research, we have examined some aspects of international law: human rights, criminal law, trade law, and arbitration.

Toronto, ON, Canada Abbas Poorhashemi

Contents

Editor and Contributors

About the Editor

Abbas Poorhashemi is the President of the Canadian Institute for International Law Expertise (CIFILE) and Editor-in-Chief of the CIFILE Journal of International Law (CJIL). He specializes in public international law, international criminal law, human rights, and international environmental law. He earned his Ph.D. in International Law from the University of Strasbourg in 2005 and completed a Postdoctoral Fellowship in International Law & Globalization at UQAM University, Canada, in 2013. Dr. Poorhashemi has taught international law for over a decade and supervised over 200 dissertations and theses. He has practiced law in various jurisdictions and has been a registered expert before the International Criminal Court (ICC) since 2023. Dr. Poorhashemi's professional affiliations include memberships in several international law associations and editorial boards. His research interests encompass international law, criminal law, environmental law, arbitration, and human rights.

Contributors

Yousra Mohamed Kamal LLM in International Commercial Law and Arbitration, Pepperdine School of Law, State Counsel, ESLA, Cairo, Egypt

Sanaz Shabani Kolahi LLM in Law of Internet Technology at Bocconi University, Milan, Italy

Izuchukwu Temilade Nwagbara Research Volunteer at CIFILE, British Nigeria Law Forum, Lagos, Nigeria

Maria Diory F. Rabajante Department of Public Law, Max Planck Institute for the Study of Crime, Security and Law, Freiburg im Breisgau, Germany

Artificial Intelligence and Human Rights

Sanaz Shabani Kolahi

1 Introduction

A key concept in considering the impacts of AI on humans and their rights is surveillance. AI makes interference and monitoring of people easy. Anybody who owns powerful and cutting-edge technologies may leverage them to control people, regardless of whether they care about human rights. AI and its related technologies, like Machine learning and the Internet of Things, offer new possibilities for modelling, processing, and exploiting large datasets, thus opening the doors to a new era of algorithmic surveillance.[1] Consequently, with such broad surveillance, undoubtedly, broad human rights violations come.

Algorithmic surveillance affects various types of human rights, including rights to non-discrimination, equality by law, fair treatment by courts, privacy, freedom of movement and residence, freedom of thought and religion, freedom of opinion and expression, right to assembly, right to democracy, right to social security, right to work, and right to education. Some are even more fragile in confrontation with technology and AI, constituting a significant risk for equal and proper implementation. Due to this fact, it is crucial to have strict boundaries to control surveillance technologies. Hence, the Geneva Declaration on Targeted Surveillance and Human Rights was drafted to address the challenges.

Surveillance is not in the traditional state for states to target mass surveillance. With the growing usage of smart devices and the Internet everywhere, the private sector must also examine preserving human rights when gathering and using data. Otherwise, their surveillance could result in vast breaches of human rights. "The

[1] Kosta (2022), p. 213.

S. S. Kolahi (✉)
LLM in Law of Internet Technology at Bocconi University, Milan, Italy

A. Poorhashemi (ed.), *Artificial Intelligence and the Future of International Law*, SpringerBriefs in Law, https://doi.org/10.1007/978-3-031-73334-5_1

mass collection of information on users by private parties is not irrelevant to the ability of public authorities to conduct surveillance programmes."[2] The public sector can obtain the data with a broad range of justifications, and it is much easier for them to use the already gathered data.

It could be alleged that, in some cases, surveillance is also beneficial, especially in the case of predictions of serious situations in a country, such as terrorist attacks or other serious crimes. However, this dangerous reasoning could result in mass and/or discriminatory surveillance. This was the integral issue in the case of La Quadrature du Net v. France, which was brought before CJEU to annul some French government regulations that mandated electronic communication providers to retain and process vast amounts of user data to combat terrorism. General and discriminatory retention of the data without the consent of the data owners was one core argument of the claimant, and it led to the court ruling precluding the national legislative measures requiring the indiscriminate retention of traffic and location data.

Adopting the AI Act in the EU has regulated some constraints that did not possess a clear legal basis until now or were sector-specific. Article 5 of the AI Act recognizes some situations in which the use of AI is prohibited. Some of them are surveillance circumstances. For example, in parts 1 (b), (c), and (g), discriminatory surveillance is prohibited. Also, in part (d), profiling with AI for criminal purposes is prohibited. Facial recognition, an effective tool for surveillance aims, is constrained under part (e) to "*create or expand facial recognition databases through the untargeted scraping of facial images from the internet or CCTV footage*". Some cases draw some exceptions to using specific AI technology but with special consideration. One case is the use of remote biometric identification only by police under the high-risk AI use conditions and fulfillment of the relevant rules. Furthermore, the authorization of the police for AI systems that process data about sensitive/ protected characteristics to label or filter.

2 Impacts of AI on Privacy

Louis Brandeis defined privacy as an individual's right to be left alone, protecting against unwanted disclosure of private facts, thoughts, and emotions.[3] Privacy is addressed in many regional and international documents, namely the Charter of Fundamental Rights of the European Union (CFREU), the Universal Declaration of Human Rights (UDHR), and the American Convention on Human Rights. One articulation of the notion of privacy is Article 12 of the International Covenant on Civil and Political Rights (ICCPR).

Privacy is not a very recent notion, and it has always been a challenge in different ways. However, with the development of AI, it has been a more serious issue as AI

[2] Rojszczak (2024), p. 63.

[3] Warren and Brandeis (1980), p. 193.

systems gather as much data as possible. Personal data or even non-personal data retention could give rise to the recognition of the individuals, which is a real danger to privacy. Privacy preservation concerning AI systems is a matter of balancing the utility and the intrusion.

All AI system creation stages, including training, testing, evaluation, and deployment, need data. Corporations are more eager to use any kind of data to build a decisive competitive system. There is no boundary for companies to collect the data. Enormous amounts of personal data, including our fingerprints, travel details, interaction with people, and medical reports, are collected, stored, processed, and profiled with the help of AI. These stages could cause privacy breaches in many shapes.

This is more problematic with big tech companies as they have many functionalities and services, and they can justify the collection and retention of big data due to their essential use, while SMEs could be more accessible to control.

The data used to sort, score, classify, evaluate, and rank people is sometimes collected without the data subject's consent. Some regulations, like the General Data Protection Regulation (GDPR), require anyone who gathers data to inform the owner and obtain consent. However, AI acts autonomously and is just a part of the structure. Data misuse is often unchallenged by those whose personal information is collected because they either cannot do so or are helpless to tackle the issue.[4]

The emergence of generative AI poses new privacy risks; it can infer personal data, create defamatory content about people, or impersonate them. Moreover, they use the input data by users in their interactions to train the system and keep them providing information in response to other users' demands. "*These systems generate predictive or creative output that, through relational inferences, can even impact people whose data was not included in the training datasets or who may never have been users of the systems themselves.*"[5]

AI has also changed group privacy. The big data available from different kinds of groups, especially the more vulnerable groups, results in their suppression in society and the diminishing of individual privacy of the members of such groups. The social scoring system in China is an obvious example of how this information can be used to control and abandon access to things like credit, housing, employment, or social services.

With AI, people are unaware of how much data their software and devices generate, process, or share. During the height of the COVID-19 pandemic, data exploitation was a severe concern due to the proliferation of contact-tracing applications. Some of these applications use AI and machine learning, including the Canadian application that used them to supplement low testing rates to develop targeted risk profiles for individuals.[6] This situation could have resulted in data exploitation since the applications' users were unaware of how the application gathered data and who

[4] Jane (2019), p. 33.

[5] King and Meinhardt (2024), p. 19.

[6] Scassa et al. (2020). p. 4.

had access to such data. Moreover, potential researchers could use this data in other AI applications.

The AI algorithms are incredibly substantial in the preservation or breach of privacy. The Google Spain case[7] has established this importance and tries to equip people with action to defend their privacy through AI algorithms. CJEU relies its ruling basis on the Data Protection Directive.[8] The court declared that under Article 12, the data subject is provided with some rights to obtain the rectification, erasure, or blocking of data when the processing is not compliant with the directive. Moreover, based on Article 14, the data subject may, at any time, on compelling legitimate grounds relating to his particular situation, object to the processing of data relating to him. This judgment was one of the first decisions that secured the position of privacy against big technology corporations' unbound use of AI.

The following case law in the EU goes beyond the objection to breach of privacy. The CJEU and ECJ try to create a safe environment for individuals by using GDPR as a powerful tool. One of the most critical cases in this regard is the Facebook case[9] before CJEU, which was brought by the Belgian DPA arguing that collecting the data of the web surfing behaviour of millions of people by cookies who have decided not to become a member of Facebook's social network is either a violation of Belgian data protection law and the override of the privacy right of people who not joined the facebook. Therefore, by this decision, the court illustrates the essence of protecting privacy against the new technologies.

One recent case targeting a particular category of individuals is the TikTok case. It was investigated under the Digital Service Act (DSA) as if it failed to design the proper privacy setting for minors. It was then established that it did not design the proper safeguard for the protection of minors.

Very recently, the AI act developed principal regulation about the privacy of individuals based on article 16 of the Treaty on the Functioning of the European Union ("TFEU"), which mandates the EU to lay down the rules relating to the protection of individuals regarding the processing of personal data. It found its way into underlying principles expressed in Recital 27, which precisely explains the privacy and data governance that AI systems are developed and used per privacy and data protection rules and high standards for data processing regarding quality and integrity. It also recalls the ethics guidelines for trustworthy AI and outlines these principles. Likewise, recital 69 established that the right to privacy and protection of personal data must be guaranteed throughout the entire lifecycle of the AI system.

All in all, using AI to gather, process, and exploit personal data poses a risk to our privacy and even can control our actions. That is why many actors use AI to access confidential information.[10]

---

[7] Case C-131/12.

[8] Directive 95/46/EC.

[9] Case C-645/19.

[10] Manheim and Kaplan (2018).

3 Impacts of AI on Jobs and Workplaces

AI can adversely affect people's work. While AI can help employees by performing specific tasks that do not require discretion or human emotion, it has the capacity to replace humans in certain types of work, thereby posing a problem to one's right to work, which various human rights covenants, including the ICCPR, recognize as a fundamental right. It also puts people in economic inequality and poor living standards. Besides this dark scenario, there are many other concerns regarding the impact of AI on work situations. Employers use AI to manage their recruiters and workplaces and adapt it for assistance in some functions. Sometimes, they use AI for employment decisions or promotions.

In the abovementioned circumstances, algorithms can systematically disadvantage workers and job applicants based on race, sex, or other characteristics. Despite being presented as neutral and objective, AI can reproduce human biases and introduce new forms of bias, depending on how such tools were built and trained.[11] Because of the incomplete data about a particular group and the biased data on which the AI is trained, those using AI systems could make discriminatory employment or hiring decisions.

Similarly, AI in the workspaces may expose employees to massive information collection, data vulnerability, and an annoying atmosphere. AI is increasingly incorporated into the workplace to monitor and track employees. Employers can record everything from their employees' health conditions[12] to task performance. The use of AI in the workplace thus poses a risk to the employees' right to privacy, especially if such use is done without the knowledge and consent of employees. Further, to the extent that the use of AI can cause an annoying atmosphere in the workplace, it jeopardizes the employees' right to just conditions of work, safe and healthy working conditions, and dignity at work.

In this regard, one document containing regulations about processing personal data in the employment context is GDPR. According to the regulations, data must be processed for specified and legitimate purposes that are proportionate and necessary. At the same time, employers must ensure that the data are adequate, relevant, and not excessive for such legitimate purposes.

There is some regulation about the workplace in the AI Act that prohibits devising systems that are able to infer the emotions of a natural person. As well, two applications refer to employment applications of AI among high-risk systems listed in Annex 3 of the act: systems that are used for the recruitment or selection of

[11] Kim and Bodie (2021), p. 294.

[12] It is important to note that the international community recognizes the right to health as a human right. The 1948 Universal Declaration of Human Rights affirms the right to health. This right includes timely access to satisfactory quality and affordable health care. As a result, realizing the right to health might appear at first sight as the main objective of international health cooperation. Several international legal instruments, including non-binding tools such as the 2015 Sustainable Development, recognized this right in international law. 1. Poorhashemi (2023), pp. 41–60. https://periodicos.unisanta.br/index.php/GHL/article/viewFile/3531/2356.

employees, targeted job advertisements, analysis and filter of job applications, and evaluation of candidates and systems for the operation of decision making affecting terms of work-related relationships, containing a range of critical management decisions including promotion, termination and performance evaluation.

4 Impacts of AI on Discrimination

Despite vital principles and regulations about non-discrimination in international documents, there is a growing concern that AI algorithms can reinforce existing biases and discrimination against different groups in society, specifically certain groups such as people of colour, women, and people with disabilities. For instance, AI-powered predictive policing systems have been criticized for perpetuating racial bias and discrimination. A 2016 investigation by ProPublica[13] found that an AI-powered system used by the United States (U.S.) justice system to predict future criminal behaviour was twice as likely to flag black defendants as future criminals compared to white defendants.

AI systems are fed with data. Big data is the primary source that any AI system uses for initial learning and continuous operation. Thus, discrimination could result from extensive data collection and analyses that codify discrimination in AI technologies, whether intentionally[14] or unintentionally. Regarding intentional discrimination, some documents clarify for the people who operate AI to assess and avoid discrimination. Namely, the "Toronto Declaration on Protecting the Right to Equality and Non-Discrimination in Machine Learning Systems", the Economic Co-operation and Development (OECD) recommendation on AI and the Draft Recommendation of Council of Europe on the Human Rights Impacts of Algorithmic Systems.

There is a potential risk for discrimination in AI as "inequality in application," in which AI can result in disproportionate impact or discriminatory treatment of certain groups without human involvement.[15] This is because longstanding patterns of discrimination are embedded in the data with which AI is trained. Therefore, it replicates them. "Correspondingly, when such systems are used to make predictions or decisions concerning individuals, they are likely to produce discriminatory outcomes."[16]

In line with the effects that an AI system could have on discrimination, the AI Act bans AI systems that use social behaviour or personal characteristics to unfairly

[13] Could be found at https://www.propublica.org/article/machine-bias-risk-assessments-in--criminal-sentencing (last visited: 28/07/2024).

[14] Tschider (2018), p. 98.

[15] Calo (2017), pp. 411–412.

[16] Vivek (2021), p. 8. Available at SSRN: https://ssrn.com/abstract=3734664.

discriminate against people in contexts unrelated to where the data was collected or in a manner that is unjustified or disproportionate.

Discrimination by AI may over or under-represent some people. As mentioned earlier, discriminatory acts of AI could be a wrong prediction based on race, and there can be discrimination against women, unequal targeted online advertising, and discrimination in translation or education for linguistic minorities.[17] AI could also possibly reinforce social inequality, as when a person who lives in a poor neighbourhood where burglaries are typical could be subjected to a higher premium for house insurance because of a high risk of a burglary.[18]

A recent case in this issue is the Schufa case. It highlights significant concerns regarding discrimination arising from the use of AI in automated decision-making. The CJEU determined that Schufa's credit scoring process, which involves profiling individuals based on personal data, can result in significant legal and economic impacts on individuals, such as loan denials. The decision underscores the importance of non-discrimination principles. Automated decision-making systems must not lead to unfair or biased treatment of individuals. The GDPR mandates that entities using such systems implement safeguards to prevent discriminatory effects and ensure fair and justifiable decisions.

5 Responsibility of States and Corporations Under International Human Rights Law Concerning AI

Both States and corporations are responsible for preserving human rights. Regarding the responsibility of States, the "Universal Declaration of Human Rights" enumerates rights and implies that states, as primary bearers of responsibility, are bound to respect, protect and fulfill human rights. Furthermore, the most crucial document about corporations is "*Norms on the Responsibilities of Transnational Corporations and Other Business Enterprises concerning Human Rights,*[19]" which obliges them to protect, respect, and remedy frameworks. It is worth mentioning that the responsibility of none of the states or corporations could be replaced by each other, clarifying Principle I of the Norms, according to which states continue to have the primary responsibility to ensure respect for human rights. The same Principle provides that companies only have responsibilities 'within their respective spheres of activity and influence'. They are complementary to each other.

Obviously, under international human rights law, both states and corporations have responsibilities to ensure that AI systems are used in a manner that respects human rights. Any general responsibility and accountability that are deemed for states and corporations must be obeyed in matters of AI, especially since there are

[17] Shabani and Jabbari (2022).

[18] Zuiderveen Borgesius (2020), p. 13.

[19] Available at: https://digitallibrary.un.org/record/501576?ln=en.

few specific international regulations about it. During the past decades, many documents have provided rules and duties for international actors to protect human rights. However, there is little documentation in the international arena concerning protecting human rights while deploying AI.

Writing about every human rights obligation of states and corporations takes pages and ages. Nevertheless, we mentioned two underlying documents which contain the responsibility to protect human rights. There are many other conventions on various subjects of human rights. To apply them per AI, we must take into account each regulation. Indeed, some norms, specifically about human rights and AI, are discussed in this book. While the specific obligations may vary depending on the context and the actors involved, some general principles can be identified from the relevant literature.

In the first place, we mention some documents that are not precisely about AI but speak about other subjects and indirectly imply some concerns about AI. General Comments on The Right to Science (general comments),[20] General Data Protection Regulation (GDPR), and United Nations High Commissioner for Human Rights in The Right to Privacy in The Digital Age are in this category.

The general comments entail in part 3 that the states have positive and negative obligations for freedom of participation, enjoyment of scientific progress, and enjoyment of the benefits of science without any discrimination. Alongside these vital elements, there are five more interrelated elements: availability, accessibility, quality, acceptability, and protection. We claim that AI is included in this entitlement of rights based on section E of part 5, which names artificial intelligence as one of the emerging technologies deriving from scientific knowledge; hence, it is under the scope of this declaration. It articulates obligations for States in these terms: "*States parties have to adopt policies and measures that expand the benefits of these new technologies while at the same time reducing their risks.*" Moreover, the detailed undertakings for States are international cooperation, taking decisions concerning the development and use of these technologies within a human rights framework, imposing the duty of human rights due diligence on non-state actors, and paying particular attention to some unique aspects of these technologies like long term job loss or ownership and control of data.

Another remarkable document in this category is GDPR. Indeed, it is mostly about privacy and data protection, but it contains some rules about automated decision-making. Article 22 prohibits unauthorized processing and profiling. GDPR is a significant development in AI since it has strict regulations and clearly places penalties for businesses developing AI, like fines for non-compliance. Automated decision-making has two conditions to make a corporation responsible for producing legal effects or similarly significant effects. There are some examples in Recital 71 and in Article 29 of 2018 opinion on automated decision-making under the GDPR by the Working Party, including someone's civil or political rights, such as

[20] E/C.12/GC/25 (General comment No. 25 (2020) on article 15: science and economic, social and cultural rights).

the freedom of association or the right to vote, immigration or citizenship determinations and rights and decisions that deny someone an employment opportunity or put them at a severe disadvantage.[21] According to the mentioned examples, the effects that could trigger the application of Article 22 affect the person's legal or contractual rights or if the effects result from exploiting some vulnerability or disadvantage.[22] Thus, corporations are responsible for their decisions by AI in human rights fields, and they are obliged to consider GDPR in these matters.

The report of the United Nations High Commissioner for Human Rights in The Right to Privacy in The Digital Age[23] focuses on the obligations of States and corporations in the privacy field. The responsibilities of States are respecting the duty to protect the right to privacy in the digital age plus putting in place adequate safeguards and effective oversight. The latter have pillars that set an overarching framework protecting against undue interference and procedural safeguards and oversight for surveillance and communications interception, which are established in part four of the report. Similarly, in part 5, some corporate responsibilities are under the broad term of responsibility to protect. This duty requires corporations to (a) avoid causing adverse impacts through their own activities; (b) avoid contributing to adverse impacts through their own activities, either directly or through some outside entity (government, business, or others); and (c) seek to prevent or mitigate adverse human rights impacts directly linked to their operations, products or services by their business relationships, even if they have not contributed to those impacts.[24] Although these responsibilities are based on guiding principles, digital rights must be considered for the document to be met. In addition, the responsibility for remedy is obligatory for both groups.

In the second place, few documents in the international arena exclusively establish the rules regarding artificial intelligence. The most influential ones are the Toronto Declaration: Protecting the Right to Equality and Non-Discrimination in Machine Learning Systems (Toronto Declaration), the Recommendation of the OECD's Council on Artificial Intelligence (OECD recommendation), UNESCO's Recommendation on The Ethics of Artificial Intelligence (UNESCO recommendation), Ethics Guidelines for Trustworthy AI (ethics guidelines) and the most recent one is AI Act which could recreate the new structure for the protection of human rights while using AI.

---

[21] Article 29 Data Protection Working Party, Guidelines on Automated individual decision-making and Profiling for the purposes of Regulation 2016/679, WP251 rev. 01, adopted on 3 October 2017/21–22.

[22] Hintze (2020), pp. 5–6. Available at SSRN: https://ssrn.com/abstract=3630026or https://doi.org/10.2139/ssrn.3630026.

[23] A/HRC/39/29. (2018). United Nations High Commissioner for Human Rights. The Right to Privacy in the Digital Age, available at: https://www.ohchr.org/en/documents/reports/ahrc3929-right-privacy-digital-age-report-united-nations-high-commissioner-human.

[24] Guiding Principle 13. See also OHCHR, (2012). "The corporate responsibility to respect human rights: an interpretive guide".

The Toronto Declaration is an essential regulation that aims to promote inclusion, diversity and equity and safeguard equality. To achieve this aim, these are the responsibilities of States and corporations: proactively prevent discrimination, comply with existing human rights laws and standards, and prevent discrimination, particularly against marginalized groups. Dedicated responsibilities are outlined for each State and corporation in line with these shared responsibilities.

On one hand, States must keep their systems updated and consider the potential risks. If any harm occurs, states must provide effective remediation and redress, conducting regular impact assessments, audits, and tests to identify the risks of systems or mitigate their harmful outcomes. States must ensure and require accountability and maximum possible transparency, which means explainability and intelligibility. In this regard, they must avoid using "black box systems" that cannot be subjected to meaningful standards of accountability and transparency. States must have diverse employment policies and ensure that active authorities in technological sectors take human rights training and that independent oversight mechanisms exist. According to the UN Committee on Economic, Social and Cultural Rights comments, states should make regulations that are compliant with human rights law to oversee the private sector.[25]

On the other hand, corporations' responsibilities primarily contain respect for human rights independent of state obligations and conformity with human rights due diligence frameworks. To clarify the due diligence, it has these three pillars: identify potential discriminatory outcomes, take effective action to prevent and mitigate discrimination, track responses, and be transparent about efforts to identify, prevent, and mitigate against discrimination. They should take action to ensure individuals and groups have access to meaningful, effective remedies and redress.

The OECD recommendation[26] aims to foster AI while ensuring respect for human rights. To realize this goal, international stakeholders adhere to the responsible use of AI in favour of human rights maintenance and implement mechanisms and safeguards for this. The other principles for actors in this recommendation are transparency and responsible disclosure, which consist of some actions; one remarkable action is enabling those adversely affected by an AI system to challenge its outcome. Actors must ensure traceability to enable an analysis of the AI system's outcomes and responses to inquiry and continuously apply a systematic risk management approach to address risks like privacy and bias. Likewise, actors are accountable for the proper function of the systems concerning human rights and the mentioned principle, and they shoulder the responsibility.

Parallely, some principles directly and specifically target the states and undertake some undertaking, including investing in and encouraging a supportive environment for AI without inappropriate bias. The states must actively cooperate with each

[25] E/C.12/GC/20. (2019). UN Committee on Economic, Social and Cultural Rights, General Comment 20, UN Doc. Para. 11.

[26] OECD/LEGAL/0449.

other and other actors regarding AI issues to maintain the balance between AI and people's labour rights.

UNESCO's recommendation[27] is among the documents which address some values and principles for using AI. Although it seems ethical considerations, there are values that states should protect, promote and respect human rights and fundamental freedoms, human dignity, and equality, ensuring diversity and inclusiveness, peace, inclusiveness, and justice, equity, and directly obliges the states to act in conformity with human rights. The recognized principles in this recommendation also point to the integral human rights that must be obeyed, which are the implementation of procedures for risk assessment and the adoption of measures to preclude harm to human rights. AI actors should promote social justice, safeguard fairness and non-discrimination in compliance with international law, and respect privacy and data protection through governance mechanisms, impact assessment, design approaches, and consistency with international law. There is a possibility of attributing ethical and legal responsibility to AI systems, for example, in cases of remedy, though they can never replace ultimate human responsibility and accountability. Moreover, transparency is essential for challenging the outcomes of the system, which may infringe on human rights and explainability that is closely related to the latter, and it is necessary to understand and trace the outcomes. Responsibility and accountability in this recommendation recall States and other actors containing corporations.

Similar to the previous recommendation, the ethics guidelines[28] enshrined some crucial principles and rules for protecting human rights while using AI, unlike the correlation of ethics and human rights established in the latter by these terms "*Respect for fundamental rights, within a framework of democracy and the rule of law, provides the most promising foundations for identifying abstract ethical principles and values, which can be operationalized in the context of AI.*"[29] The five fundamental rights which are mentioned as a basis for the trustworthy use of AI in this guideline are respect for human dignity, freedom of the individual from any intervention, respect for democracy, justice and the rule of law, equality, non-discrimination, and solidarity.

The Council of Europe Framework Convention on Artificial Intelligence and Human Rights, Democracy, and the Rule of Law establishes clear obligations for states and corporations to preserve human rights within the rapidly evolving AI landscape. States are required to implement comprehensive regulatory frameworks that ensure AI systems respect and uphold human rights, democracy, and the rule of law. This includes mandating transparency, accountability, and fairness in AI development and deployment. Corporations, conversely, are obliged to adhere to these regulations by conducting thorough human rights impact assessments, ensuring

---

[27] SHS/BIO/PI/2021/1.

[28] Adopted by High-Level Expert Group on Artificial Intelligence established by the European Commission.

[29] Ethics guidelines for trustworthy AI, P. 9.

ethical AI practices, and maintaining robust oversight mechanisms. Both states and corporations must work collaboratively to prevent AI technologies from infringing on fundamental rights, such as privacy, freedom of expression, and non-discrimination, thereby fostering a secure and equitable digital environment for all individuals.

6 AI Act Obligations

The most important innovation of the AI act is categorizing the AI systems based on risks that they may pose. According to each system specification, the operators of these systems must take steps to comply with the regulations and make their system safe and human-centric.

Some systems have such an unacceptable risk that they are prohibited from being used. Article 5 explains in detail which systems are deemed to have unbearable risk. Among them are social scoring systems, untargeted facial recognition systems, real-time biometric identification systems, and emotion detection systems.

The next level of systems in AI are marked as high-risk and are prone to pose a significant risk of harm to the health, safety, or fundamental rights of natural persons, including by not materially influencing the outcome of decision-making. This part is heavily regulated, and actions are required to secure its use. The providers of AI systems must comply with all the requirements of the AI Act and other relevant applicable laws in their sectors.

Most vital obligations regarding high-risk systems are stated in articles 9 to 15 under section 2 of the Act, including risk management systems, data governance, technical documentation, record-keeping, transparency, human oversight and accuracy, robustness, and cybersecurity.

The AI Act also addresses the general purpose of AI models as systems that could have systematic risk and be considered high-risk systems. GPAI models present systemic risks when the cumulative amount of computing used for its training is more significant than 1025 floating point operations (FLOPs). They could pose risks either by themselves or their integration into other systems.

To minimize their risk, the providers of these systems are required to update their technical documentation, draw up, keep up-to-date, and make available information and documentation to providers of AI systems who intend to integrate the GPAI model into their AI systems. Specifically, the mandatory obligation for the GPAI with systemic risk is model evaluation according to standard protocols, risk assessment, and cyber security protection. Another essential obligation for the providers of the GPAI is the preservation of copyrights of contents they use, especially during the training.

It has some provisions that strive to make a safe environment for humans in interaction with AI and tries to strengthen the position of human beings against AI. Transparency obligation is one of them. AI systems that interact with humans, generate deepfakes or are used for biometric identification are subject to transparency requirements. Users must be informed when interacting with an AI system, and specific disclosures must be made about the nature of the system and the data it processes. Moreover, The AI Act emphasizes the importance of human agency and control over AI systems. It requires that AI systems be designed to augment human decision-making rather than replace it, ensuring that humans retain control and can override decisions made by AI when necessary.

To be effective, the AI Act also makes the providers liable and accountable, and they must be accountable for the deployment and outcomes of these systems. This includes ensuring compliance with the AI Act's provisions and being liable for any harm caused by the AI systems.

7 Conclusion

In conclusion, the impact of AI on human rights is a growing concern as AI makes it easier to monitor and interfere with people's lives, potentially leading to human rights violations. Surveillance, a key concept in considering the impacts of AI on human rights, has opened the doors to a new era of surveillance, named algorithmic surveillance, which could lead to broad human rights violations. AI significantly impacts privacy, jobs and workplaces, and discrimination. AI violates the right to work by replacing humans and can reproduce human biases or introduce new forms of bias. Discrimination by AI can result in disproportionate impact or discriminatory treatment of certain groups without human involvement, potentially leading to discriminatory outcomes. It is crucial to address these concerns to avoid violating human rights and to ensure that AI is used ethically and responsibly.

Several documents outline the responsibilities of States and corporations when protecting human rights in the context of AI. These documents emphasize the importance of transparency, accountability, oversight, and the need for human agency and the protection of fundamental rights. While the specific responsibilities may vary depending on the context and the actors involved, these documents provide a valuable framework for ensuring that AI systems are used in a way that respects human rights. In details:

States have the following responsibilities:

Legislation and Regulation States have a duty to create and enforce laws that ensure AI systems respect human rights. This may involve regulating the development, deployment, and use of AI and providing guidelines on ethical and human rights considerations.[30]

Due Diligence States should conduct due diligence to ensure that AI systems used or supported by the government respect human rights. This may involve assessing

[30] Ebers (2019), p. 46.

AI systems' potential human rights impacts and taking steps to prevent or mitigate any adverse effects.

Access to Remedy States should ensure that those affected by human rights abuses involving AI can access effective remedies, including judicial and non-judicial mechanisms.

Promoting Human Rights in International Cooperation States should promote human rights in their international dealings related to AI, such as by encouraging other states and international organizations to adopt human rights-based approaches to AI governance.

Corporations also have the following responsibilities:

Respect Human Rights Corporations are responsible for respecting human rights, which means they should avoid causing or contributing to human rights abuses through their AI systems. This involves conducting human rights due diligence, identifying potential risks, and preventing or mitigating adverse impacts.

Policy Commitment Corporations should have a publicly available policy commitment to respect human rights in AI, which should be communicated to relevant stakeholders, including employees, business partners, and the public.

Transparency and Accountability Corporations should be transparent about their AI systems, including how they are developed, deployed, and used.[31] This may involve disclosing the data and algorithms used and the measures taken to ensure that AI systems respect human rights.

Remedy Corporations should provide or cooperate in providing remedies to individuals and communities affected by human rights abuses linked to their AI systems. This may involve participating in grievance mechanisms or supporting access to judicial or non-judicial remedies.

Both States and corporations have international human rights law responsibilities to ensure that AI systems respect and promote human rights. These responsibilities involve creating and enforcing legislation, conducting due diligence,[32] providing access to remedies, and promoting transparency and accountability.

The AI Act significantly alters the obligations of states and corporations regarding the preservation of human rights in AI usage. For states, the Act mandates establishing and enforcing comprehensive legal frameworks to regulate AI systems, ensuring they protect human rights. It requires robust oversight mechanisms for regular monitoring and compliance and transparency and accountability measures to ensure AI developers disclose relevant information. States must also conduct

[31] Fjeld et al. (2020), p. 28.

[32] Raso et al. (2018).

human rights impact assessments to evaluate and mitigate the potential adverse effects of AI systems.

The AI Act introduces stringent risk management frameworks for corporations to identify and mitigate risks associated with AI. Corporations are required to ensure data quality and integrity, avoid biases, and protect individuals' privacy. To maintain transparency, they must provide detailed information about their AI systems, including training data and decision-making processes. The Act also mandates human oversight to ensure AI decisions can be overridden when necessary and establishes effective remedial mechanisms to address grievances and provide remedies for AI-related human rights abuses. Overall, the AI Act aims to create a safer and more ethical AI ecosystem, requiring active protection and promotion of human rights by both states and corporations in AI development and deployment.

References

Calo R (2017) Artificial intelligence policy: a primer and roadmap. UC Davis Law Rev 51:399–435

Ebers M (2019) Regulating AI and robotics: ethical and legal challenges. In: Ebers M, Navarro SN (eds) Algorithms and law. Cambridge University Press, Cambridge. (chapter 2)

Fjeld J, Achten N, Hilligoss H, Nagy A, Srikumar M (2020) Principled artificial intelligence: mapping consensus in ethical and rights-based approaches to principles for AI. Berkman Klein Center Research Publication No. 2020–1

Hintze M (2020) Automated individual decisions to disclose personal data: why GDPR Article 22 Should Not Apply. Available at SSRN: https://ssrn.com/abstract=3630026 or https://doi.org/10.2139/ssrn.3630026

Jane SA (2019) Artificial intelligence: a threat to privacy? Nirma Univ Law J 8(2):21–36

Kim P, Bodie M (2021) Artificial intelligence and the challenges of workplace discrimination and privacy. ABA J Labor Employment Law 35:289. Washington University in St. Louis Legal Studies Research Paper No. 21–09-02, Saint Louis U. Legal Studies Research Paper No. 2021–26, 289–235

King J, Meinhardt C (2024) Rethinking privacy in the AI era, Policy Provocations for a Data-Centric World, White Paper. Stanford Institute for Human-Centered Artificial Intelligence, Stanford

Kosta E (2022) Algorithmic state surveillance: challenging the notion of agency in human rights. Regulation & Governance 16:212–224

Manheim K, Kaplan M (2018) Artificial intelligence: risks to privacy and democracy. Yale Journal of Law and Technology 21:106. Loyola Law School, Los Angeles Legal Studies Research Paper No. 2018–37, 107–188

Poorhashemi A (2023) Global Health law and human rights. Global Health Law J Brazil 1(1):41–60. https://periodicos.unisanta.br/index.php/GHL/article/viewFile/3531/2356

Raso F, Hilligoss H, Krishnamurthy V, Bavitz C, Kim L (2018) Artificial intelligence & human rights: opportunities & risks. Berkman Klein Center Research Publication No. 2018–6

Rojszczak M (2024) Bulk surveillance, democracy and human rights law in Europe: a comparative perspective, 1st edn. Routledge, London. https://doi.org/10.4324/9781003449263

Scassa T, Miller J, Bronson K (2020) Privacy, ethics, and contact-tracing apps. In: Flood CM, MacDonnell V, Philpott J, Thériault S, Venkatapuram S (eds) Vulnerable: the law and policy of COVID-19. University of Ottawa Press, Ottawa. Ottawa Faculty of Law Working Paper No. 2020-23

Shabani S, Jabbari N (2022) The impacts of technology on the Human rights of linguistic minorities, Sanaz Shabani, Niki Jabbari, Specialusis Ugdymas/Special Education. 1 (43)

Tschider C (2018) Regulating the IoT: discrimination, privacy, and Cybersecurity in the artificial intelligence age. Denv Univ Law Rev 96:87

Vivek K (2021) AI and human rights law. In: Martin-Bariteau F, Scassa T (eds) Artificial intelligence and the law in Canada. LexisNexis Canada, Toronto, p 8. Available at SSRN: https://ssrn.com/abstract=3734664

Warren S, Brandeis L (1980) The right to privacy. Harv Law Rev 4:193

Zuiderveen Borgesius FJ (2020) Strengthening legal protection against discrimination by algorithms and artificial intelligence. Int J Human Rights:1–22

Artificial Intelligence and International Criminal Law

Izuchukwu Temilade Nwagbara

1 Introduction

Another issue crucial in the relationship between AI and international law is the intricacies of human warfare that have evolved across centuries, both in the justification for warfare and the conduct of warfare. As knowledge of science and technology advances, the sophistication of weapons of war does likewise.[1] The effect of such advancement in the sophistication of weapons has been vast and conspicuous. For instance, the airspace and underwater have now become terrains for warfare. Likewise, improvements in weapons and weapons systems have led to a greater capacity for military casualties during battles. It has been argued, for instance, that the casualties of the participants of World War 1 dwarfed those of previous wars, considering the short span of the war; these were due to the advanced technology of weapons.[2]

While some sovereign nations attempted to draw up military codes guiding the conduct of their military during the war,[3] it became necessary for the international community to conglomerate to canonize established and recognized laws and customs of war to maintain a modicum of humanity in the conduct of war. The canonization efforts have led to treaties such as the first Geneva Convention of

[1] Mallik (2004).

[2] Showalter and Royde-Smith (2023). John Mueller argues that the Taiping rebellion, a civil war that raged in China probably resulted in more death casualties in absolute terms. However, the Taiping rebellion lasted between 1851–1864, 13 years as opposed to 4 years of World War I; Mueller (1991), p. 4.

[3] Carnahan, B.M. *The Lieber Code*. Essential Civil War Curriculum. www.essentialcivilwarcurriculum.com/the-lieber-code.html.

I. T. Nwagbara (✉)
Research Volunteer at CIFILE, British Nigeria Law Forum, Lagos, Nigeria

A. Poorhashemi (ed.), *Artificial Intelligence and the Future of International Law*, SpringerBriefs in Law, https://doi.org/10.1007/978-3-031-73334-5_2

1864[4]—ultimately replaced by the Geneva Convention of 1949 on the same subject—the Hague Conventions of 1899 and 1907,[5] the four Geneva Conventions of 1949 and their additional protocols. At the end of World War II, which witnessed mass atrocities and gross violations of the laws of war, modern international criminal law regimes emerged to ascribe individual criminal responsibility for crimes under international law.[6]

Ever since the pioneering tribunals of modern international criminal law, that is, the Nuremberg tribunal and the Tokyo tribunal, international criminal law has progressed, moving from the creation of ad-hoc tribunals to the establishment of a permanent tribunal, the International Criminal Court ('ICC'), to try international crimes defined by its statute, the Rome Statute of the International Criminal Court ('Rome Statute').

Notwithstanding establishing a permanent international criminal law regime, humankind's thirst for conflict appears insatiable. The arms race, never abating, has taken a new dimension: artificial intelligence. AI is being mooted for application in military operations, particularly weapons systems, which would have legal implications. This section examines the intricacies and implications of the nexus between artificial intelligence and international criminal law.

2 AI: Weapons Systems and Legal Responsibility

AI is a branch of computer science specializing in creating and managing technology that can learn to autonomously make decisions and carry out actions on behalf of a human being.[7] AI is a simulation of human intelligence processes by machines, especially computer systems.[8] An example of an AI process already in use is speech recognition, an AI application that allows an intelligent system to convert human speech into text or code.[9] This is something that would ordinarily require a human to transcribe into text. AI systems seek to carry out actions and make decisions that require human intelligence.

AI is being touted for use in any capacity that requires human intelligence. Unsurprisingly, its proposed uses are not limited to civilian use. Military organizations seek to develop AI systems to bolster military capacity and for possible deployment in conflict. The types of AI systems used, and the extent to which they are deployed in conflict situations raise legal and social questions. There are

[4] Convention for the Amelioration of the Condition of the Wounded in Armies in the Field, signed 22 August 1864.

[5] Signed on 29 July 1899 and 18 October 1907 respectively.

[6] Principles of International Law Recognised in the Charter of the Nurnberg Tribunal and in the Judgment of the Tribunal. (1950). *Yearbook of the International Law Commission*, vol. II, para. 97.

[7] Rouse (2023), p. 3.

[8] Burns (2023).

[9] Rouse (2023).

questions as to what extent AI systems should be deployed in conflict situations; should they be deployed for physical combat, or should they be restricted to intelligence, surveillance, and reconnaissance (ISR)?[10] There is the question of the possibility of a human loop in the control of the decision-making process of AI—a mixture of the processing capabilities of AI with human oversight.[11] The foremost legal question in the minds of scholars is who takes responsibility for damages and casualties resulting from the autonomous decision of AI systems.

3 AI and the Law of Armed Conflict

One cardinal principle of the law of armed conflict (LOAC) is the principle of distinction, which entails that those partaking in hostilities must distinguish between combatants and civilians, and they may only target combatants or those taking active part in hostilities in the conduct of military action.[12] In the Advisory Opinion on the *Legality of the Threat of Nuclear Weapons*, the International Court of Justice affirmed that it is an "intransgressible principle of international customary law" that states must never make civilians the object of attack and, consequently, must never use or deploy weapons that are incapable of distinguishing between civilian and military targets.[13] Thus, if AI weapons systems like robotics or Lethal Autonomous Weapons Systems (LAWS) are employed for physical combat, there is the question as to whether the AI systems could adequately distinguish between combatants and civilians.

Undoubtedly, there is an onus on the combatants of the opposing sides to distinguish themselves from civilians by their apparel.[14] Nonetheless, AI systems deployed for combat must be trained to identify and distinguish combatants. AI systems are trained with large volumes of data,[15] and it is expected that insignias of various national armed forces might be fed into the systems to train them to recognize and distinguish possible combatants of those armed forces. As such, AI systems might have no problems identifying and distinguishing combatants in international armed conflicts.

A quandary, however, arises in the category of non-international armed conflicts (NIACs)—which form the bulk of modern armed conflicts—wherein there are no established insignias for the existing and prospective non-state armed groups. In international humanitarian law, there is no combatant status for non-state armed

[10] Danks (2020).

[11] Cristiano et al. (2023), p. 3.

[12] Melzer (2014), p. 296; See also Common Article 3 of the Geneva Conventions of 1949.

[13] Legality of the Threat or Use of Nuclear Weapons. Advisory Opinion of 8 July 1996. International Court of Justice. https://www.icj-cij.org/sites/default/files/case-related/95/095-19960708-ADV-01-00-EN.pdf.

[14] Melzer (2014), p. 296.

[15] Danks (2020).

groups in NIACs, and there is also no onus on members of organized armed groups taking an active part in hostilities to distinguish themselves by an insignia. Nonetheless, common Article 3 of the Geneva Conventions, which deals with NIACs, protects those who do not actively participate in hostilities. This dicey state of distinction in NIACs poses a challenge for soldiers of recognized armed forces. This may serve as an incentive for the recognized armed forces of a state to deploy AI weapons systems, instead of human soldiers, to the battlefield, as it is easy for soldiers of armed forces to be targets of non-state armed groups whilst it being difficult for soldiers to identify members of non-state armed groups or those actively taking part in hostilities. AI is thus desirable for deployment in enemy-controlled or contested areas since those environments are the riskiest for soldiers in NIACs.[16]

However, how can AI weapons systems deployed for physical combat in NIACs distinguish those who actively take part in hostilities from those who do not actively take part in hostilities in the absence of insignias? Would AI systems like robots be trained to respond only if initially attacked by humans? If so, AI systems would be precluded from self-informed pre-emptive strikes in self-defence, which might remove the military advantage a party seeks to gain by deploying AI. What would constitute an "attack" by humans, and what kind of response would the AI systems give to such an "attack"? Suppose an exuberant young boy sees a robot in a conflict area and mischievously begins to throw stones at the robot. Would the robot be able to assess the boy as just a flippant and recalcitrant child and make an informed decision to refrain from responding to the "attack" of the boy, as is expected of a human soldier?[17] If five women, enraged by the contemporaneous lethal actions of the robot on clan members who actively took part in hostilities, throw stones at the robot, would the robot deem that a legitimate attack worthy of a riposte or would it be able to refrain from retaliating? These real-life conflict-related intricacies, with profound legal implications, are the severe considerations to be had in the discussions related to the training and possible deployment of autonomous AI weapons systems in conflict situations, particularly in NIACs where it is pretty difficult to distinguish those taking active part in hostilities.

On the flip side, the argument is that improved technology, including AI systems with improved targeting capacities, can help further the cause of distinction during an armed conflict. Since the First Gulf War and its use of cruise missiles, weapons' advanced targeting ability has been discussed.[18] For instance, uncrewed aerial vehicles (UAVs) such as weapons drones can be used for intelligence, surveillance, target acquisition, and reconnaissance. They can be used to identify hideouts of rebel forces and monitor the movements of rebel forces or leaders who are cogent targets for elimination. Thus, if such weapons drones can accurately delineate and distinguish the enclave of an enemy target from the nearby civilian abodes, it might be argued that such weapons systems should be utilized to carry out elimination strikes

[16] Cristiano et al. (2023), p. 5.

[17] Florence (2009).

[18] Anderson (2009), p. 331.

as the target is precise, distinguished from civilian objects, and does not require risking soldiers for a physical operation. However, a contention arises as to whether such weapons drones should be able to make the strike decision by themselves as an AI system or whether it should be human operators, viewing the situation via a monitor, making that decision. Would AI systems be able to apply intricate discretion? If, after identification of the hideout of the rebel leader and a decision to strike, two children hawking fruits walk into the hideout to sell their goods to the rebels, would the AI weapons systems be able to apply discretion to halt the attack pending when the children leave, or would it proceed with the attack and make the children collateral damage? Does it even understand the concept of collateral damage and the principle of proportionality that might serve to excuse civilian casualty in proportion to the lawful military advantage? These considerations constitute the conundrum in the interface between AI and LOAC.

4 AI Weapons Systems and Responsibility (State and Individual)

Having examined possible legal intricacies and implications arising from the deployment and use of AI weapons systems, it is pertinent to examine the issue of responsibility or liability. On the one hand, States' responsibility for grave breaches of international humanitarian law, which materialize when utilizing AI weapon systems, is mooted. On the other hand, international criminal law concerns itself with individual criminal responsibility.

States that toy with the idea of AI weapons systems have had to grapple with the issue of responsibility for their deployment. In this context, the AI weapons systems adorn the appellation—Lethal Autonomous Weapons Systems (LAWS). So far, the efforts of research towards the development of LAWS have been initiated and funded by States—the enormous funding and research effort might go beyond the realms of individual capacity[19]—and it behooves that the issue of responsibility for the actions of LAWS begins with States.

Admittedly, States seem to be aware of the portending danger of LAWS—they nonetheless do not abate in their efforts to develop LAWS—and have conglomerated to fashion out a framework of principles for the development and usage of LAWS. As a corollary to the 1980 United Nations Convention on Certain Conventional Weapons (CCW), France initiated discussions in 2014 to respond to LAWS's potential development and utilization challenges.[20] In 2016, state parties to the CCW decided to establish an open-ended Group of Governmental Experts on

[19] Dawes (2021) and Doward (2018).

[20] *11 Principles on Lethal Autonomous Weapons Systems (LAWS)*. France Diplomacy. https://www.diplomatie.gouv.fr/en/french-foreign-policy/united-nations/multilateralism-a-principle-of-action--for-france/alliance-for-multilateralism/article/11-principles-on-lethal-autonomous-weapons-systems-laws.

emerging technologies in the area of LAWS (GGE on LAWS) at the fifth CCW review conference.[21] The GGE on LAWS improved the informal meeting of experts convened according to a mandate of a meeting of state parties to the CCW in 2013.[22]

Following extensive deliberations, the GGE on LAWS formulated the *"Guiding Principles affirmed by the Group of Governmental Experts on Emerging Technologies in the Area of Lethal Autonomous Weapons System,"* which were adopted at the 2019 meeting of the state parties to the CCW.[23] These guiding principles have also been endorsed by the so-called "Alliance for Multilateralism" spearheaded by France and Germany.[24] France and Germany prepared a political declaration on LAWS, framing the guiding principles as "11 principles on Lethal Autonomous Weapons Systems."[25]

The guiding principles, while not binding or conclusive on the subject as they were affirmed without prejudice to the result of future discussions, were formulated to address potential challenges posed by emerging technologies in LAWS. The guiding principles, thus, purport to be the railings guiding the research efforts toward building LAWS technologies. On the relevant topic of responsibility, I affirm that international humanitarian law (IHL) shall apply to all weapons systems, including the potential development and use of LAWS. As such, state responsibility for breaching IHL principles in using LAWS is possible.[26]

Principle II affirms that human responsibility for decisions on the use of weapons systems must be retained since accountability cannot be transferred to machines. In essence, if international crimes result from the decisions/actions of LAWS, principle II affirms that individual criminal responsibility should arise. While this principle proffers some form of protection against the dangers of LAWS by ascribing responsibility to humans, its practical application is convoluted and dicey. The ascription of individual criminal responsibility requires a mental element just as much as the material elements of the crime. Article 30 of the Rome Statute provides that to be criminally responsible (and consequently liable for punishment), the person must have committed the material elements with intent and knowledge.

Proving the material elements of any underlying acts of core international crimes committed by LAWS while challenging is attainable. However, proving the mental

---

[21] *GGE on lethal autonomous weapons systems*. The Digital Watch. https://dig.watch/processes/gge-laws.

[22] Ibid.

[23] *Guiding Principles affirmed by the Group of Governmental Experts on Emerging Technologies in the Area of Lethal Autonomous Weapons System*. https://www.ccdcoe.org/uploads/2020/02/UN-191213_CCW-MSP-Final-report-Annex-III_Guiding-Principles-affirmed-by-GGE.pdf.

[24] *Critical Commentary on the "Guiding principles"*. (2019, November).

[25] The declaration was opened for endorsement at the Alliance for Multilateralism event on 26 September 2019. *11 Principles on Lethal Autonomous Weapons Systems (LAWS)*. France Diplomacy. https://www.diplomatie.gouv.fr/en/french-foreign-policy/united-nations/multilateralism-a-principle-of-action-for-france/alliance-for-multilateralism/article/11-principles-on-lethal-autonomous-weapons-systems-laws.

[26] Sassoli (2002), p. 401.

element is a conundrum. The two factors for the mental element are "intent" and "knowledge." Can LAWS appreciate knowledge of core international crimes and the underlying acts of those crimes? Can it appreciate and delineate situations that constitute international crimes, and can it distinguish them from situations that do not? If LAWS cannot grasp the purport of the above posers, can it really be said to know about international crimes as a basis for committing the crime? If LAWS cannot grasp the knowledge of international crimes, by default, it definitely cannot have the intent to commit international crimes. Another philosophical conundrum lurks, which is that if LAWS can grasp the intricate knowledge of international crimes and can choose to have intent—the presence of intent denotes the capacity to choose to have or not to have intent—to commit international crimes, can such weapons systems indeed be said to be autonomous or merely pre-programmed (by human-computer scientists) to be able to appreciate the basic legal contours of international crimes? Only time will tell. If it does become possible for LAWS to have intent and knowledge to commit international crimes by its own cognitive processes, which individual(s) would take responsibility for the crimes committed by LAWS? The computer scientists that built the systems (hardware and software)? Are the humans responsible for the physical maintenance of the systems? Or the military and political leaders responsible for commissioning the development and usage of LAWS? If principle II is to be taken to its logical conclusion, then the military and political leaders responsible for commissioning the development and usage of LAWS should be ascribed individual criminal responsibility for international crimes resulting from the actions of LAWS.

Another issue regarding individual criminal responsibility for LAWS actions is the mode of liability involved. Since LAWS takes the decisions/actions through its autonomous cognitive processes, it is a direct perpetrator. Because humans had no input—in a purely autonomous decision—nor full control over the decision and action, it would not be legally possible to deem humans as co-perpetrators, indirect perpetrators, or indirect co-perpetrators under Article 25 of the Rome Statute. Thus, superior responsibility under Article 28 of the Rome Statute might be the next point of call as regards the mode of liability. Article 28 ascribes individual criminal responsibility to military commanders or persons effectively acting as military commanders for crimes committed by forces under their effective command/authority and control due to their failure to exercise control properly over such forces. The responsibility arises where the military commander either knew or, owing to circumstances at that time, should have known that the forces were committing or about to commit such crimes and that the military commander or person failed to take all reasonable measures within their power to prevent or repress their commission or to submit the matter to the competent authorities for investigation and prosecution. The first factor to be determined in the superior responsibility mode is whether the military commanders or persons effectively acting as military commanders have effective command/authority and control over the forces committing the crime. Concerning LAWS, the military commander or person must have effective command/authority and control over LAWS.

Is it possible to have effective command/authority over an autonomous weapons system? Does such an autonomous weapons system have a component that makes room for a human loop of control? If so, does that make such a system genuinely autonomous or semi-autonomous? If the decision-making process of the weapons system has no human element or input, then it could be said to be fully autonomous, which begs the question — does a weapons system need to be fully autonomous to constitute LAWS? Would semi-autonomous weapons constitute LAWS? These intricacies would need to be considered in determining the factor of effective command/authority and control under the superior responsibility mode of liability.

The second factor under superior responsibility mode is knowledge of the commission of the crime; the military commander or person must know or, owing to the circumstances at the time, should have known that the forces were committing or about to commit such crimes. With the autonomous and recursive nature of LAWS, it behooves to highlight that its internal cognitive process, as well as the decision-making process, is not only not subject to prognosis with exactitude, but it is not open for deliberation with external forces; this is assuming that the weapons system in question is fully autonomous with no human loop embedded. Thus, while it is possible to know when the LAWS is committing crimes for which, at that point, the military commander or person can no longer prevent its commission, the chances that a military commander or person must have known that an LAWS deployed in combat, is about to commit international crimes are bleak.

The last factor entails that the military commander failed to take all necessary and reasonable measures within their power to prevent or repress their commission or to submit that matter for investigation and prosecution. As stated earlier, the lack of privity in the internal processes of the LAWS makes it almost impossible to prevent the commission of the crime. Repression comes in after the commission has started. Considering the lack of privity in the internal decision-making process and the enormous damage that can ensue from the deployment and usage of LAWS, should there be an obligation for developers of LAWS to put in place a mechanism to repel a LAWS that is acting irrationally swiftly, some form of ex-post control in the absence of ex-ante control?

Having discussed the difficulties ascribing a mode of liability for individual criminal responsibility under Articles 25 and 28 of the Rome Statute, perhaps a *sui generis* mode of liability for individual criminal responsibility can be created. Such a mode of liability could create strict liability for the political and military leaders responsible for commissioning the creation and deployment of the LAWS, who have now committed grievous crimes. The strict liability of leaders for crimes committed by LAWS might appear harsh on the surface. Still, it might serve to place a heavy burden on the political and military leaders of nations actively seeking to develop LAWS for deployment and usage, representing to them that they would be the ones to bear responsibility for their military technology adventures/fantasies.

5 AI and International Criminal Trials

The international criminal justice process seeks individual criminal responsibility for atrocities which constitute international crimes. It seeks to end impunity for the perpetrators of the most severe crimes of concern to the international community and thus contribute to the deterrence/prevention of such crimes.[27] It has been argued that failure to address impunity serves as an impetus for repeated atrocities.[28]

The process of bringing alleged perpetrators of international crimes to account for their crimes is quite onerous. The prosecutor has the burden to prove the guilt of the accused beyond reasonable doubt.[29] The standard of proof applies to the material elements (chapeau elements and underlying acts) as well as the mental elements of the crime. This high standard of proof places a significant evidentiary burden on the prosecutor. Unlike domestic prosecution, wherein the police and investigating team have free reign—within the bounds of the law—and the total weight of the law behind them to investigate and gather evidence for international crimes, prosecution and investigation teams of international criminal tribunals must conduct cross-border investigation and are dependent on the cooperation of the state where the crimes were committed. Thus, in cases where international crimes are alleged to have been committed by senior officials of the state, less or hostile cooperation by the state might be the case. Further, pending the entry of the international prosecution and investigation teams into the territory of the state, crucial documents and pieces of evidence could have been destroyed or subdued.[30]

There has been a quest for alternative means of investigating and gathering crucial evidence for prosecution in international criminal trials. Whilst the traditional on-ground investigations remain indispensable, potent alternative means are desirable. Social media and smartphones have resulted in an unprecedented volume of online videos; a culture of impulsive urge to record and upload videos seems ubiquitous. Thus, it is possible that while atrocities were being perpetrated, someone or some persons recorded and uploaded online or simply streamed the event; in an act of impunity, perpetrators themselves sometimes post videos and pictures on social media. This deluge of pictures and videos online can be a great source of digital evidence for prosecuting atrocities—open-source investigations. For instance, videos posted to social media contributed to the basis for seeking an arrest warrant in the Al-Werfalli case in the context of the Libya situation at the ICC.[31]

However, sorting out valuable pieces of evidence from this deluge and analyzing them to get specific information can be onerous or impossible for humans. This is where AI comes in. Face recognition AI systems might be utilized to identify

[27] Preamble to the Rome Statute.

[28] Nwagbara (2023), p. 78.

[29] Article 66 of the Rome Statute.

[30] After Japan's surrender during World War II, tons of documents that could have been relevant for the prosecution of the Japanese leadership hierarchy were destroyed. Dittrich et al. (2020), p. 183.

[31] Irving (2017).

victims or suspected perpetrators from a deluge of pictures uploaded online. Voice recognition AI might be utilized to identify the voices of victims or suspected perpetrators in an anonymous recording to carry out the task. Whilst open-source investigation opens up an alternative means of acquiring evidence of atrocities, analyzing the pool of evidence might prove difficult or almost impossible with AI tools.

Open-source investigation of digital evidence has its own concerns, particularly with regard to the fair trial rights of defendants.[32] Nonetheless, the combined efforts of open-source investigation and AI analyzing tools can contribute immensely to international criminal trials.

6 Conclusion

The advancement of science and technology has brought positive gains to the world. It has also rapidly improved the capacity for more significant warfare casualties through growing weapon sophistication. AI is a growing field of computer science which seeks to improve human processes' efficiency on a phenomenal level drastically; this improved efficiency offered by AI is sought for weapons systems by states and stakeholders in the military-industrial complex. The military application of AI, particularly in weapons systems such as LAWS, elicits various legal intricacies and complications. It has been argued that the scramble to exploit emerging technologies for military use has accelerated faster than efforts to assess the dangers they pose and whatever limits their use.[33] Should AI weapons systems be deployed for physical combat? Would AI weapons systems deployed for physical combat be able to satisfy the IHL principle of distinction? Would AI weapons systems be able to satisfy the IHL principle of proportionality? Would AI weapons systems be able to apply discretion ordinarily expected of a soldier? These and many more are legal considerations to be had. At this stage, there are more questions than answers.

States seem to be at the forefront of research efforts to develop and use LAWS. Thus, State responsibility for the grave breaches of IHL by actions of LAWS should be in the offing. A general concern about LAWS is whether these weapons find their way into the hands of non-state/terrorist armed groups.[34] With the sophistication required in developing LAWS, it is implausible that non-state armed groups build LAWS from scratch as opposed to acquiring them. Thus, who takes responsibility for the acquisition of LAWS by non-state/terrorist groups? Would states and stakeholders of the military-industrial complex be willing to maintain an international register of AI weapons systems produced so as to track the provenance of LAWS easily?

[32] Zarmsky and Moinki (2023).

[33] Hirsh (2023).

[34] Lewis (2023), p. 967.

Whilst principle II of the guiding principles of GGE on LAWS affirms human responsibility for actions of LAWS as accountability cannot be ascribed to machines, the current modes of liabilities in the Rome Statute might make it technically impossible to ascribe individual criminal responsibility for international crimes resulting from the actions of LAWS. Thus, a *sui generis* mode of liability is proposed: strict liability of political and military leaders responsible for commissioning the development and usage of LAWS. With such strict liability, ascription of individual criminal responsibility is possible.

Finally, the application of AI in analyzing digital evidence during open-source investigations is an area that needs further attention. In as much as the defendants' fair trial rights are catered to, such an application can aid the international criminal justice process.

References

Anderson K (2009) The rise of international criminal law: intended and unintended consequences. Eur J Int Law 20(2):331–358

Burns E (2023) Artificial Intelligence (AI). TechTarget www.techtarget.com/searchenterpriseai/definition/AI-Artificial-Intelligence

Carnahan BM. The Lieber Code. Essential Civil War Curriculum. www.essentialcivilwarcurriculum.com/the-lieber-code.html

Cristiano F, Broeders D, Delerue F, Douzet F, Gery A (eds) (2023) Artificial intelligence and international conflict in cyberspace. Routledge, London. https://doi.org/10.4324/9781003284093

Critical Commentary on the "Guiding principles" (2019, November) Article 36. https://article36.org/wp-content/uploads/2019/11/Commentary-on-the-guiding-principles.pdf

Danks D (2020) How adversarial attacks could destabilize military AI systems. IEEE Spectrum. https://spectrum.ieee.org/adversarial-attacks-and-ai-systems

Dawes J (2021) UN fails to agree on 'killer robot' ban as nations pour billions into autonomous weapons research. The Conversation. https://theconversation.com/un-fails-to-agree-on-killer-robot-ban-as-nations-pour-billions-into-autonomous-weapons-research-173616

Dittrich VE, Von Ligen K, Osten P, Makraiova J (eds) (2020) The Tokyo tribunal: perspectives on law, history and memory. TOAEP, Dubai. https://www.toaep.org/nas-pdf/3-dittrich-lingen-osten-makraiova

Doward J (2018) Britain funds research into drones that decide who they kill, says report, the Guardian. https://www.theguardian.com/world/2018/nov/10/autonomous-drones-that-decide-who-they-kill-britain-funds-research

Florence C (2009) Rolling stone—soldier gets rocked by stone throwing Afghan crowd. Defense Visual Information Distribution Service. www.dvidshub.net/news/42683/rolling-stoned-soldier-gets-rocked-stone-throwing-afghan-crowd

GGE on lethal autonomous weapons systems. The Digital Watch. https://dig.watch/processes/gge-laws

Guiding Principles affirmed by the Group of Governmental Experts on Emerging Technologies in the Area of Lethal Autonomous Weapons System. https://www.ccdcoe.org/uploads/2020/02/UN-191213_CCW-MSP-Final-report-Annex-III_Guiding-Principles-affirmed-by-GGE.pdf

Hirsh M (2023) How AI will revolutionize warfare. Foreign Policy. https://foreignpolicy.com/2023/04/11/ai-arms-race-artificial-intelligence-chatgpt-military-technology/

Irving E (2017) And so it begins…social media evidence in an ICC arrest warrant. OpinioJuris. http://opiniojuris.org/2017/08/17/and-so-it-begins-social-media-evidence-in-an-icc-arrest-warrant/

Legality of the Threat or Use of Nuclear Weapons. Advisory Opinion of 8 July 1996. International Court of Justice. https://www.icj-cij.org/sites/default/files/case-related/95/095-19960708-ADV-01-00-EN.pdf

Lewis DA (2023) War crimes involving autonomous weapons: responsibility, liability and accountability. J Int Criminal Justice 21(5):965–980. https://doi.org/10.1093/jicj/mqad027

Mallik A (2004) Technology and security in the 21st century: a demand-side perspective (Report no. 20). Stockholm International Peace Research Institute, Stockholm, p 4. www.sipri.org/sites/default/files/files/RR/SIPRIRR20.pdf

Melzer N (2014) The principle of distinction between civilians and combatants. In: Clapham A, Gaeta P (eds) The Oxford handbook of international law in armed conflict, pp 296–331. https://doi.org/10.1093/law/9780199559695.003.0012

Mueller J (1991) Changing attitudes towards war: the impact of the first world war. Br J Polit Sci 21(1):4

Nwagbara IT (2023) Impunity: an impetus for repeated atrocities—Nigerian Army as a case study. CIFILE J Int Law 4(7):62–79. https://doi.org/10.30489/cifj.2023.378065.1060

Principles on Lethal Autonomous Weapons Systems (LAWS). France diplomacy. https://www.diplomatie.gouv.fr/en/french-foreign-policy/united-nations/multilateralism-a-principle-of-action-for-france/alliance-for-multilateralism/article/11-principles-on-lethal-autonomous-weapons-systems-laws

Rouse M (2023) Artificial Intelligence. Dent Tech. www.techopedia.com/definition/190/artificial-intelligence-ai

Sassoli M (2002) State responsibility for violations of international humanitarian law. Int Rev Red Cross 84:401

Showalter DE, Royde-Smith JG (2023) World War I: 1914–1918. Encyclopaedia Britannica. www.britannica.com/event/World-War-I/The-end-of-the-German-war

Zarmsky S, Moinki J (2023) Symposium on fairness, equality, and diversity in open source investigations: out in the open: fair trial rights and open source evidence at the ICC. OpinioJuris. http://opiniojuris.org/2023/02/10/symposium-on-fairness-equality-and-diversity-in-open-source-investigations-out-in-the-open-fair-trial-rights-and-open-source-evidence-at-the-icc/

Artificial Intelligence and International Trade Law

Maria Diory F. Rabajante

1 Introduction

Technological advances have always impacted trade—from the introduction of steam to the invention of computers. As the world is now on the cusp of the fourth industrial revolution, or Industry 4.0, AI significantly transforms how trade is conducted, who conducts trade, and what is being traded.[1] Unlike other technologies, AI is usually characterized by a high level of autonomy, making it challenging to categorize AI systems for regulatory purposes. Thus, AI's legal implications are more complex than those of other digital technologies. Accordingly, examining whether the existing legal landscape still adequately covers cross-border trade involving AI is crucial.

This chapter explores the intersection between AI and international trade law and maps out the relevant rules that govern and affect transnational trade with AI components. It begins with setting the context by discussing the impact of AI on cross-border trade and explaining why this should be considered a separate, albeit related, matter from the impact of digital technologies in general. It then examines the extent to which the current laws cover trade with AI components and analyzes whether such laws are sufficient to address the challenges posed by AI. The chapter reveals that the existing trade laws do not adequately address such challenges. It summarizes the opportunities and challenges international trade law faces in the contemporary society affected by AI.

---

[1] World Trade Organization (2018).

M. D. F. Rabajante (✉)
Department of Public Law, Max Planck Institute for the Study of Crime, Security and Law, Freiburg im Breisgau, Germany
e-mail: m.rabajante@csl.mpg.de

A. Poorhashemi (ed.), *Artificial Intelligence and the Future of International Law*, SpringerBriefs in Law, https://doi.org/10.1007/978-3-031-73334-5_3

2 How, Who, and What: AI's Impact on International Trade

Concerning *how* trade is conducted, AI has impacted the operations and supply chain management. AI systems help forecast demand fluctuations, optimize inventory levels, identify bottlenecks, and streamline logistics. Walmart, for instance, uses AI to analyze customer preferences and buying behaviour and enable all of its thousand suppliers around the world to monitor inventory on a real-time basis.[2] The use of AI in transportation likewise aids in reducing trade costs. With machine learning algorithms, a long-distance trucking system could predict the arrival of trucks and detect the petrol stations where drivers should refuel, thereby reducing travel time.[3] As regards customs compliance, the most basic communications technologies streamline procedures and hence reduce the costs of cross-border trade, while the more advanced AI-based applications are used to monitor and comply with regulatory rules.[4]

The proliferation of AI-based machine translation solutions also affects trade conduct. Machine translations are used as production inputs, such as when conducting market surveys and establishing good relationships with existing and prospective clients.[5] In the financial sector, AI-based risk assessment tools help evaluate a prospective borrower's creditworthiness. This makes it easier for financial institutions to render more accurate decisions efficiently. AI systems are likewise used to detect fraud and analyze the interconnectedness between borrowers, facilitating financial institutions' management of their lending portfolios.[6]

AI systems positively impact those *who* conduct trade as these technologies help connect freelance service providers with clients from various parts of the world. This gives people from developing countries the opportunity to earn income through providing services remotely to companies located in developed countries. The decline in trade costs also benefits micro, small, and medium-sized enterprises, as well as companies in developing countries. On this note, the World Trade Organization (WTO) estimates that the share of developing countries in global trade will increase from 46% to 57% by 2030.[7]

Finally, using AI changes *what* is being traded, as shown by the composition of trade in services and goods. The current digital infrastructure supplies services electronically or through communication networks. The reduction in transportation costs likewise leads to an increase in the trade of time-sensitive products, such as life-saving medical supplies and perishable food products.[8] Further, because of the proliferation of AI-based applications, it is now possible to trade works created with

[2] Roden et al. (2017), pp. 936–937.

[3] World Trade Organization (2018), p. 66.

[4] Lim (2021).

[5] Ferencz et al. (2022).

[6] OECD (2021).

[7] World Trade Organization (2018), p. 117.

[8] World Trade Organization (2018), p. 90.

AI. Generative AIs like Midjourney, Stable Diffusion, and DALL-E can be used to create artwork, and applications using GPT-4 can be used to generate any text, such as articles or essays.

3 Distinctive Features of Trade with AI Components

The third industrial or digital revolution brought computers, microprocessors, cell phones, and the internet. In contrast, the fourth industrial revolution goes beyond digitalization; it fundamentally transforms the technological landscape. It introduces new technologies, including AI, that fuse the digital, physical, and biological worlds, thus impacting all disciplines and even challenging our understanding of what it means to be human.[9]

While there is yet a consensus on the emergence of artificial general intelligence (AGI), *i.e.*, a fully autonomous system that is as advanced as a human, the current AI systems may already be described as having a high level of autonomy in their decisions and actions.[10] For instance, autonomous vehicles can now drive without human input. There are also automated legal advice tools (ALATs), sometimes called robot lawyers, which can act as legal chatbots, review documents, generate smart contracts, or help provide legal advice through data analytics.[11]

With the increasing prevalence of autonomous technology, the legal implications are becoming more complex. In an accident due to a technical glitch in an autonomous vehicle, an issue arises regarding whether the driver, the vehicle owner, the manufacturer, or the AI system should assume the liability. The emergence of ALATs sparks the debate on whether they are involved in law practice and should, therefore, be subject to a code of professional responsibility.[12] Moreover, the extent of autonomy that AI systems have and will have in the future raises the question of how they should be classified for regulatory purposes—should they be treated as legal persons, tools, or non-biological autonomous agents, or should a new category be created for them?[13] As explained below, AI systems challenge the traditional distinction between goods and services in the WTO law and raise the question of whether the current intellectual property (IP) laws are sufficient to promote technological innovation. Clearly, the impact of AI on international trade must be considered distinct, though related, from that of digital technologies in general.

---

[9] World Economic Forum (23 July 2023).

[10] Liu and Lin (2020), p. 419.

[11] Bennett et al. (2018).

[12] Garner (2017).

[13] Liu and Lin (2020), p. 419.

4 AI and International Trade Law Framework

After the Second World War, attempts were made to form an International Trade Organization (ITO), which would be a partner to the World Bank and the International Monetary Fund. However, the ITO never existed due to concerns that it might encroach on domestic sovereignty.[14] Instead, the General Agreement on Tariffs and Trade (GATT), which was intended to be provisional as a prelude to the ITO, became the institutional basis for the international trade regime. In 1995, the WTO was established as an umbrella organization that includes the GATT. The WTO provides a forum for the Member States to negotiate agreements aimed at reducing trade obstacles. The WTO agreements, also called WTO trade rules or WTO law, resulted from such negotiations. They cover goods (through the GATT), services (through the General Agreement on Trade in Services or the GATS), and IP (through the Agreement on Trade-Related Aspects of Intellectual Property Rights or the TRIPS Agreement).

5 Trade in Goods and Services

The GATT applies to trade in goods, while the GATS applies to trade in services defined under four modes of supply, *i.e.*, Mode 1 (cross-border supply), Mode 2 (consumption abroad), Mode 3 (commercial presence), and Mode 4 (presence or movement of natural persons).[15] Both the GATT and the GATS adopt a broad rule of non-discrimination, which is enshrined in two principles, *i.e.*, the Most Favored Nation (MFN) principle and the National Treatment principle. The MFN principle requires each Member State to grant to like goods or services of any other Member State treatment no less favourable than it accords to like goods or services of any other state.[16] On the other hand, the National Treatment principle requires each Member State to treat goods or services of any other Member State on an equivalent footing as domestic goods or services.[17]

Although it is clear that the GATT and the GATS govern the international trade of goods and services, technological advancements have blurred the traditional distinction between goods and services.[18] This distinction is important because while the GATT and the GATS require compliance with the MFN and National Treatment principles, they have different scopes and guarantee different commitments. Whereas the GATT ensures free market access as its general principle, the GATS has a positive list approach that obliges Member States to accord non-discriminatory

[14] Trebilcock and Trachtman (2020).

[15] GATS, Art. I.

[16] GATT, Art. I; GATS, Art. II.

[17] GATT, Art. III; GATS, XVII.

[18] Burri (2015); Weber (2021), pp. 54–69.

treatment only in the service sectors and the modes of supply listed in their GATS Schedules.[19] The goods-services distinction thus implies radically different obligations.

6 Digital Products: Goods or Services?

Products purchased online but delivered physically undeniably fall within the scope of the GATT.[20] However, the emergence of e-commerce over the last two decades made it difficult to classify different types of "digital products." There have been debates on whether products such as downloaded or streamed film or music, e-books, software, and e-tickets call for applying the GATT or the GATS.[21] Part of the difficulty in classifying these products is the lack of clear definitions of the terms "good" and "service" in the GATT and the GATS.

Some attempts were made to solve the issue. The WTO Work Programme on Electronic Commerce endeavoured to answer whether digitally delivered content products are goods or services and should, therefore, be governed by either the GATT or the GATS. The U.S. argued that these products are goods since they are inseparable from a physical medium and are not necessarily consumed after being viewed or listened to, unlike in the case of services.[22] The U.S. further stated that electricity, akin to digitally delivered content in terms of form and shape, has been treated as good ever since the GATT came into effect.[23] In stark contrast, the European Communities (EC) argued that "*[e]lectronic deliveries consist of supplies of services*"[24] and that any subsequent transformation process, *e.g.*, saving the content into a physical medium, is not connected to the initial cross-border trade and therefore does not change the digital content's intangibility.[25] Ultimately, this effort to classify digitally delivered content resulted in a deadlock.[26]

Even the Comprehensive and Progressive Agreement for Trans-Pacific Partnership (CPTPP) that provides for a definition of the term "digital product" refuses to specify whether such is a good or a service. The CPTPP expressly states that the definition therein "*should not be understood to reflect a Party's view on whether trade in digital products through electronic transmission should be categorized as trade in services or trade in goods.*"

[19] Weber (2015), p. 332.

[20] *Ibid.*, p. 325; Fleuter (2016).

[21] *See e.g.*, Weber (2015), Liu and Lin (2020) and Fleuter (2016).

[22] Wunsch-Vincent (2006b), p. 56.

[23] Wunsch-Vincent (2006b), p. 56.

[24] World Trade Organization (2000), p. 3, https://docs.wto.org/dol2fe/Pages/SS/directdoc.aspx?filename=Q:/S/C/W183.pdf&Open=True.

[25] Wunsch-Vincent (2006b), p. 60.

[26] Wunsch-Vincent (2006b), pp. 48–49.

In the *US-Gambling* case, the WTO Appellate Body concluded that online gambling and betting services are within the scope of Mode 1 of the GATS.[27] While this ruling confirmed the applicability of the GATS to services supplied electronically, the Appellate Body only assessed Mode 1 commitments and did not address, as it was not requested to, the differences between Mode 1 and Mode 2 as regards their applicability to electronically delivered services.[28] This case thus failed to answer questions regarding the exact applicability of the GATS to electronic delivery of services, as well as the classification of various types of digital products.

The *US-Gambling*'s most significant progress, which is its clarification that the WTO rules apply to e-commerce and electronically supplied services, was confirmed by the Appellate Body in *China - Publications and Audiovisual Products.*[29] In this subsequent case, the Appellate Body determined that "*where the content of a film is carried by physical delivery materials, [China's Film Regulation] will inevitably regulate who may import goods for the plain reason that the content of the film is expressed through, and embedded in a physical good.*"[30] This statement does not necessarily mean that a film is indeed a good, but rather that it includes a good to the extent that it is contained in a physical medium.[31] However, it leaves open the question of whether the trade of digitally delivered content products, such as music or e-books, is a trade in goods, services, or both.

7 AI and the Legal Gaps in the GATT and the GATS

The emergence of AI makes it even more challenging to classify items based on the goods-services regime in the WTO law. Take ALATs as an example. Are ALATs merely tools for searching legal information, or are they legal service providers? Does the use of ALATs in conducting due diligence and drafting legal documents call for applying the GATT, the GATS, or both? If the ALAT is contained in a physical medium, like in the case of *China - Publications and Audiovisual Products*, is it governed by the GATT even though it is intended to provide services such as document review and drafting of legal documents? If it is covered by the GATS instead, under which mode should it be classified? Answering these questions is not a straightforward matter.

According to a recent report of OpenAI, GPT-4 "*exhibits human-level performance on various professional and academic benchmarks, including passing a*

[27] *United States — Measures Affecting the Cross-Border Supply of Gambling and Betting Services*, WT/DS285/AB/R (2005), §215.

[28] Wunsch-Vincent (2006a), p. 326.

[29] Wunsch-Vincent and Hold (2015), p. 182.

[30] *China — Publications and Audiovisual Products* (2009), WT/DS363/AB/R, §188.

[31] Conconi and Pauwelyn (2011).

simulated bar exam with a score around the top 10% of test takers."[32] Assuming this to be true and given the debates as to whether AI systems should be capable of being accorded legal personality,[33] it is important to examine the implications of such status on the applicability of the current WTO rules. For instance, if a robot travels to another state to provide legal advice and perform other legal services, does the robot's legal personality mean that it cannot be considered a good, thereby rendering the GATT inapplicable? Since this case involves providing services, the GATS appears applicable. However, it also seems that this case does not fit in any of the four modes of supply of trade in services under the GATS.

Mode 1 is clearly inapplicable because this case does not involve a supply of services from one state to another. Mode 2 is likewise inapplicable as this case does not contemplate a situation where a service consumer goes to another state to obtain a service. Mode 3 also appears to be inapplicable since this mode requires establishing a commercial presence in another state. Finally, Mode 4 is inapplicable because this mode involves the presence of a natural person in another state to provide a service. This mode would have been applicable in the example if the robot were a natural person. However, it is not, and its legal personality does not make it a natural person.

There are proposals to add a "Mode 5" in the GATS. This new mode is meant to cover services incorporated into goods that are traded across borders[34] and would thus cover AI systems embedded in physical goods. If the robot in the example above is considered a good and therefore covered by the GATT, the addition of Mode 5 in the GATS would also bring the robot within the ambit of the GATS. Adding this mode to the GATS will also make the GATS applicable to other products with AI systems embedded in them, such as autonomous vehicles and machineries embedded with advanced technology. While the GATT covers goods with services embedded with them, it may not sufficiently address the complexities associated with these services. Having Mode 5 in the GATS that specifically recognizes these services can help in reducing non-tariff barriers, *e.g.*, regulatory discrepancies, that obstruct market access for goods with service components. However, the notion of Mode 5 is still in its infancy, and its scope and boundaries are still unclear.[35]

The use of AI also poses difficulty in determining a state's compliance with its commitments under the WTO rules. Imagine a scenario wherein a foreign insurance provider with a presence in the importing state uses AI to automate insurance coverage decisions. If the importing state bans automated decision-making for insurance coverage decisions, an argument could be made that the restriction is a violation of the importing state's market access commitments as it is a limitation on the number of providers in the form of numerical quotas, falling under the scope of Article

[32] OpenAI (2023).

[33] *See e.g.*, Novelli et al. (2022), pp. 194–219; Filipova and Koroteev (2023), pp. 359–386.

[34] Foltea (2018).

[35] *Ibid.*, p. 12.

XVI:2 of the GATS.[36] Nevertheless, it is difficult to answer whether the importing state in this example also violated the National Treatment principle by favouring domestic insurance providers that do not use AI to automate decisions. To address this issue, it is necessary to establish the "likeness" between the AI-based insurance service and the non-AI-based insurance service because the National Treatment principle applies only to the extent that a foreign service or supplier is "like" the domestic one. This would then require an inquiry into the applicability of the "technological neutrality" principle in trade law. This principle is usually taken to mean that electronically supplied services should be treated "like" those not supplied electronically[37] because the mechanism by which services are provided, *e.g.*, offline, online, or over the phone, etc., have no impact on their treatment under WTO law.[38] Unfortunately, there is still no settled definition of technological neutrality, and the WTO adjudicating bodies have yet to clarify its exact applicability, making it unclear whether this should be accepted as a general principle.[39] While some argue that it could make current rules adaptable to changing realities, others contend that it could also cause uncertainty in the event of unforeseen technological developments.[40]

8 Intellectual Property

The TRIPS Agreement is an international agreement that sets the minimum standards to which WTO Member States' domestic IP laws must conform. Like the two WTO agreements discussed above, the TRIPS Agreement contains National Treatment[41] and MFN[42] principles.

As AI systems are becoming more advanced and capable of generating works with minimal human intervention, it is crucial to ask whether the TRIPS Agreement should be readjusted to align with the evolving technological landscape. AI's emergence raises the question of whether AI-generated works should be granted IP protection and whether an AI may be designated as the IP rights holder. Connected to these questions is the issue of whether an AI is merely a tool, a legal person, or some other autonomous agent.

[36] Chander (2021), p. 125; *US-Gambling*, § 239.

[37] Weber (2015); Kwak (2022); Wunsch-Vincent (2006a).

[38] World Trade Organization (2018), p. 170.

[39] Kwak (2022).

[40] Shadikhodjaev (2021).

[41] TRIPS Agreement, Art. 3.

[42] TRIPS Agreement, Art. 4.

9 Patent

Under Article 27(2) of the TRIPS Agreement, Member States may exclude certain inventions from patentability if necessary to protect *ordre public* or morality. Since the exclusions are defined at either the national or regional level, what is considered not patentable in one country may be considered patentable in another. For instance, while Article 52 of the European Patent Convention (EPC) provides that "programs for computers" cannot be regarded as patentable inventions "*to the extent to which a European patent application or European patent relates to such subject-matter or activities as such*," there is no similar provision under the U.S. patent law. Thus, if an AI software meets the U.S. statutory requirements for patentability, it may be argued that such a program is patent eligible in the U.S. However, with respect to those states that are signatories to the EPC, software is not patentable unless it is established that the European patent application does not relate to the software "as such." The lack of uniformity in rules regarding patentability could result in forum shopping, where companies actively search for jurisdictions with laws that favour protecting their inventions or the inventions generated by their AI systems.[43]

While the TRIPS Agreement is intended to promote technological innovation, it appears that many states are reluctant to grant patent protection to AI-generated inventions. Recently, Stephen Thaler's patent applications for inventions created by an AI called DABUS, *i.e.*, Device Autonomous Bootstrapping of Unified Sentience, were denied in some countries. The U.S. Patent Trademark Office (USPTO) denied the patent application (Application No.: 16/524,350 for "Devices and Methods for Attracting Enhanced Attention") on the ground that the term "inventor" under the U.S. patent law must be a natural person and could not be broadly construed to cover a machine. The USPTO relied on U.S. case law holding that states and corporations cannot be considered inventors and applied a plain reading of the words "whoever," "individual," "himself," and "herself" in the U.S. patent law.[44] The Federal Circuit affirmed the USPTO's ruling, emphasizing that the U.S. patent law expressly provides that inventors are "individuals," and that individuals are human beings.[45] The U.S. Supreme Court denied Thaler's petition for certiorari assailing the Federal Circuit's ruling.

The European Patent Office (EPO) also refused the applications (EP18275163 for "Food Container" and EP18275174 for "Devices and Methods for Attracting Enhanced Attention"), declaring that the designation of inventor in said applications does not meet the requirements laid down in the EPC.[46] The applications for

---

[43] Mercurio and Yu (2021).

[44] USPTO (2020). *In Re Application of Application No.: 16/524,350.*

[45] *Thaler v. Vidal*, No. 21–2347 (Fed. Cir. 2022).

[46] European Patent Office (2022). *European Patent Register, EP About this file: EP3563896.* https://perma.cc/69PN-9A29, European Patent Office (2022). *European Patent Register, EP About this file: EP3564144.* (2022), https://perma.cc/PP5D-BSJ6.

inventions created by DABUS were similarly denied in the United Kingdom,[47] Australia,[48] and New Zealand[49] because only natural persons can be inventors.

Taking a different approach, the South African Companies and Intellectual Property Commission granted the patent application for "Food Container and Devices and Methods for Attracting Enhanced Attention" (ZA2021/03242) on 24 June 2021, with DABUS listed as the inventor.[50] This marks the world's first patent with an AI listed as its inventor.

Meanwhile, in Germany, the German Patent and Trademark Office (*Deutsches Patent- und Markenamt*) denied the patent application, and this denial was affirmed by the German Federal Patent Court (*Bundespatentgericht*). Nevertheless, the latter declared that the patent applicant, *i.e.*, Stephen Thaler, may be designated as the inventor in the patent application, thereby signifying the possibility of granting a patent to an AI-generated invention with a natural person as the patent owner.[51]

10 Copyright

One of the most fundamental doctrines in copyright law is that for an artistic work to be considered copyrightable, it must comply with the requirement of "originality."[52] The relevant question is thus whether an AI-generated literary or artistic work complies with this requirement, making it eligible for copyright protection.

Some jurisdictions interpret originality as connected to human creativity, suggesting the approach of not extending copyright protection to works created by non-humans. For instance, in the landmark case of *Naruto v. Slater*, the U.S. District Court for the Northern District of California rejected the argument that Naruto, a macaque, should be considered the copyright owner of the selfies he took using a wildlife photographer's unattended camera (the "Monkey Selfies").[53] Filing the case as a "next friend"[54] to Naruto, the People for the Ethical Treatment of Animals (PETA) argued that the publication of the Monkey Selfies violated Naruto's copyright. The district court rejected this and declared that the Monkey Selfies could not

---

[47] *Thaler v Comptroller-General of Patents, Designs and Trade Marks* [2023] UKSC 49 (20 December 2023).

[48] *Commissioner of Patents v Thaler* [2022] FCAFC 62, Federal Court (Full Court) (Australia).

[49] *Thaler v Commissioner of Patents* [2023] NZHC 554 [17 March 2023].

[50] CIPC (2021). Patents. *Patent Journal,* 54(7). https://iponline.cipc.co.za/Publications/PublishedJournals/E_Journal_July%202021%20Part%202.pdf.

[51] Kim (2022).

[52] Abrams (1992), Ramalho (2022) and Rosati (2018).

[53] *Naruto v. Slater*, U.S. District Court for the Northern District of California, Case No. 15-cv-04324-WHO, Order Granting Motion to Dismiss dated 28 January 2016.

[54] A "next friend" is a person who represents another who is unable to maintain a suit on his or her own behalf.

be considered Naruto's original works of authorship because the concept of authorship only extends to humans.

Relying on *Naruto*[55] and other cases emphasizing the necessity for human authorship in copyright, the U.S. Copyright Office refused to register the copyright claim in the two-dimensional artwork entitled "A Recent Entrance to Paradise" generated by an AI called Creativity Machine.[56] The application to register the copyright claim was filed by Stephen Thaler, the same person who sought patent protections for the inventions created by DABUS. Thaler challenged the U.S. Copyright Office's decision, but the U.S. District Court for the District of Columbia affirmed the denial of the copyright application and underscored that "*[h]uman authorship is a bedrock requirement of copyright*."[57]

The Singapore Court of Appeal took a similar approach in *Asia Pacific Publishing Pte Ltd v. Pioneers & Leaders (Publishers) Pte Ltd*,[58] a case involving information and database compilations. In said case, the Court declared that "*[w]ithout the identification of a human author from whom the work originated, there could be no 'original work' capable of copyright protection.*"[59] In another case, *Telstra Corporation Limited v. Phone Directories Company Pty Ltd.*,[60] the Full Federal Court of Australia held that copyright could not subsist in Yellow Pages and White Pages telephone directories as they were created through a computer-automated system and, therefore, did not allow any independent intellectual contributions from humans. The Court held that the term "originality" requires the demonstration of "*some independent intellectual effort or sufficient effort of a literary nature.*"[61] Similarly, in *Acohs Pty. Ltd. v. Ucorp Pty*,[62] the Full Federal Court of Australia emphasized the importance of human authorship. In this case, the Court held that data sheets created by a computer program were not copyrightable as a human did not create them.

Meanwhile, the Supreme People's Court in China ruled in *Tencent Co., Ltd v. Shanghai Yinxun Technology Co., Ltd.* that an article generated using Dream Writer, an AI writing tool, is copyrightable. However, the Court clarified that Dream Writer could not be considered the author in this case as it was merely a tool that assisted

[55] The Review Board of the U.S. Copyright Office cited *Naruto v. Slater*, No. 16-15469 (9th Cir. 2018), which affirmed the district court's ruling.

[56] Review Board of the U.S Copyright Office (2022). Re: Second Request for Reconsideration for Refusal to Register A Recent Entrance to Paradise (Correspondence ID 1-3ZPC6C3; SR # 1-7100387071). https://perma.cc/PVU2-9NAS.

[57] *Thaler v. Perlmutter et al*, No. 1:2022cv01564 - Document 24 (D.D.C. 2023).

[58] *Asia Pacific Publishing Pte Ltd v. Pioneers & Leaders (Publishers) Pte Ltd* (2011) SGCA 37. Singapore Law Reports (Singapore Court of Appeal).

[59] §82.

[60] *Telstra Corporation Limited v. Phone Directories Company Pty Ltd.* (2010) FCAFC 149.

[61] §102.

[62] *Acohs Pty Ltd v. Ucorp Pty Ltd*, (2012) FCAFC 16.

in writing the article.[63] Thus, the *Tencent* case still acknowledges the importance of human involvement in granting copyright protection to works created using AI.

The above cases can be contrasted with the approach in the U.K., where the copyright protection of AI-generated works could be justified under the Copyright, Designs and Patents Act 1988 (CDPA). Pursuant to Section 9(3) in relation to Section 178 of the CDPA, a computer-generated work without a human author may be granted copyright protection, with the "*person by whom the arrangements necessary for the creation of the work are undertaken*" being considered the author of such computer-generated work. Like in the U.K., the copyright laws of Hong Kong, Ireland, and India allow the protection of computer-generated works, with the person who caused the work to be created being considered as the author.[64] Nevertheless, determining who the copyright holder should be in these jurisdictions where AI-generated works appear to be copyrightable remains difficult. While these jurisdictions consider the person who caused the work to be created as the author, a question arises as to whether this person is the AI programmer or the AI user.

Parenthetically, none of the preceding cases and laws categorically supports the view that an AI may be considered a copyright holder. It would seem problematic to allow an AI to own a copyright over a work since the term of copyright protection is typically determined in reference to the author's lifetime. Using this standard would be difficult if the author is an AI.

11 Trade Secrets

Due to the insufficiency of patent and copyright laws in fully protecting AI outputs, technology companies turn to laws on trade secrets to protect their algorithms and training data.[65] To increase IP protections for technology companies, some states used trade agreements to strengthen the protection of source codes. For instance, the U.S. introduced provisions in the Trans-Pacific Partnership Agreement prohibiting the Contracting States from having regulations requiring the disclosure of a software's source code as a condition for importing, distributing, selling, or using such software.[66] However, there are concerns that provisions such as this may sacrifice the effective regulation of AI and thwart efforts towards transparency and accountability in the use of source codes, algorithms, and training data.[67] In addition, this may also reinforce the market power of already dominant technology companies.[68]

---

[63] Liang (2022).

[64] Hong Kong's Copyright Ordinance, §11(3); Ireland's Copyright and Related Rights Act 2000, §21(f); India's Copyright Act 1957, §2(d).

[65] Jones (2023), p. 75.

[66] *Ibid.*; Trans-Pacific Partnership Agreement, Art. 14.7.

[67] Jones (2023), p. 75; Słok-Wódkowska and Mazur (2022).

[68] Jones (2023), p. 81.

12 Conclusion

The above discussion shows that while AI positively impacts how trade is conducted, who conducts trade, and what is traded, it also poses complex legal implications requiring careful consideration. The current trade laws, which were drafted at a time when AI systems were not as advanced as they are today, are not sufficient to address the challenges these technologies pose. Even before using AI in the field of trade, legal scholars had already been grappling with the distinction between goods and services in determining the WTO Member States' legal obligations. This classification puzzle is far from being resolved, and the proliferation of AI systems that are likewise difficult to categorize—as tools, persons, or autonomous agents—makes the problem even more complex.

With the current state-of-the-art in AI, there is still no AGI that is fully autonomous, and therefore, it is arguable that while it is now possible to create works and inventions using AI, such creation still needs some human intervention.[69] Nevertheless, this still raises the question of how much human intervention should be considered in determining the copyrightability and patentability of works and inventions created using AI systems. Further, one needs to ask whether an AI is merely a tool, a person, or an autonomous agent before resolving the issues of whether AI-generated works deserve IP protection and whether an AI may become an IP rights holder.

Another issue that deserves attention is the digital divide between states with technological power and those that do not have such power. States with technological power dominate the markets and even the normative space. Developing states, conversely, are merely rule-takers rather than rule-makers and do not have high-tech companies that develop advanced AI systems that can be used in international trade.[70] The use of AI in trade may exacerbate this digital divide.

Considering the abovementioned challenges, policymakers must think outside the box and not simply attempt to solve new problems using old rules drafted when the current problems were still unthinkable. These challenges must be viewed as an opportunity to create a new trade regime that would address the obstacles posed by new technologies, bridge the digital divide, and address the winner-takes-all dynamics in trade. For instance, policymakers may consider accommodating "*[s]ofter, market-based, private/hybrid, multilateral, and experimental governance initiatives*" in dealing with AI-related trade issues.[71] As industry best practices, multistakeholder institutions, and private standards are commonplace in the digital world, it may be worthwhile to consider them in developing new international legal norms and reimagining new global trade regimes.[72]

[69] Ramalho (2022).

[70] Peng et al. (2021).

[71] Liu and Lin (2020), p. 448.

[72] Weber (2021).

Finally, the intersection of AI and international trade presents an opportunity for international cooperation to facilitate investment in human capital and address knowledge gaps. Some international organizations have already developed programs to help developing countries maximize the benefits of new technologies. The United Nations Conference on Trade and Development has a "TrainForTrade" programme that offers courses and skills training and supports developing states in crafting e-commerce and investment policies.[73] Similarly, the International Telecommunications Union and the International Labor Organization initiated the "Digital Skills Campaign," which is aimed at investing in the development of digital skills in the youth to increase their employability.[74] To harness the benefits of AI and ensure that international trade benefits all, policymakers and global leaders must act together, address the winner-takes-all dynamics, and create a level playing field.

References

Abrams H (1992) Originality and creativity in copyright law. Law Contemp Probl 55(2):3–44

Bennett J, Miller T, Webb J, Bosua R, Lodders A, Chamberlain S (2018) Current state of automated legal advice tools. networked society institute working paper. https://doi.org/10.13140/RG.2.2.17230.51520

Burri M (2015) The international economic law framework for digital trade. Zeitschrift für Schweizerisches Recht 135(II):10–72

Chander A (2021) Artificial intelligence and trade. In: Burri M (ed) Big data and global trade law. Cambridge University Press, Cambridge, pp 115–127

Conconi P, Pauwelyn J (2011) Trading cultures: appellate body report on China–audiovisuals (WT/DS363/AB/R, adopted 19 January 2010). World Trade Rev 10(1):95–118

Ferencz J, López-González J, Oliván Garcia I (2022) Artificial intelligence and international trade: some preliminary implications: OECD trade policy paper no. 260. OECD Publishing, Paris

Filipova I, Koroteev VD (2023) Future of the artificial intelligence: object of law or legal personality? J Digital Technol Law 1(2):359–386

Fleuter S (2016) The role of digital products under the WTO: a new framework for GATT and GATS classification. Chic J Int Law 17(1):153–177

Foltea M (2018) How to Include 'Mode 5' services commitments in bilateral free trade agreements and at multilateral stage? https://perma.cc/C9X4-Q393

Garner S (2017) Artificial intelligence and its not-so-artificial legal ethics implications. https://perma.cc/LAH8-9XDV

Jones E (2023) Digital disruption: artificial intelligence and international trade policy. Oxf Rev Econ Policy 39(1):70–84

Kim D (2022) The paradox of the DABUS judgment of the German Federal Patent Court. GRUR Int 71(12):1162–1166

Kwak D (2022) No more Strategical neutrality on technological neutrality: technological neutrality as a bridge between the analogue trading regime and digital trade. World Trade Rev 21(1):18–32

Liang I (2022) IP in China: Key cases from 2021 and the outlook for 2022. https://perma.cc/NFS2-WAFM

[73] UNCTAD, *TrainForTrade*, https://perma.cc/B43Q-J79Q.

[74] ITU, *ILO-ITU Digital Skills Campaign*, https://perma.cc/TB3J-UV5Y.

Lim AH (2021) Trade rules for industry 4.0. In: Peng S, Lin C, Streinz T (eds) Artificial intelligence and international economic law. Cambridge University Press, Cambridge, pp 97–120
Liu H, Lin C (2020) Artificial intelligence and global trade governance: a pluralist agenda. Harv Int Law J 61(2):301–344
Mercurio B, Yu R (2021) Convergence, complexity and uncertainty: artificial intelligence and intellectual property protection. In: Peng S, Lin C, Streinz T (eds) Artificial intelligence and international economic law. Cambridge University Press, Cambridge, pp 139–154
Novelli C, Bongiovanni G, Sartor G (2022) A conceptual framework for legal personality and its application to AI. Jurisprudence 13(2):194–219
OECD (2021) Artificial intelligence, machine learning and big data in finance: opportunities, challenges, and implications for policy makers
OpenAI (2023) GPT-4 technical report. https://arxiv.org/pdf/2303.08774v6
Peng S, Lin C, Streinz T (2021) Artificial intelligence and international economic law: a research and policy agenda. In: Peng S, Lin C, Streinz T (eds) Artificial intelligence and international economic law. Cambridge University Press, Cambridge, pp 1–26
Ramalho A (2022) Intellectual property protection for AI-generated creations: Europe, the United States, Australia and Japan. Routledge, Taylor & Francis Group, London
Roden S, Nucciarelli A, Li F, Graham G (2017) Big data and the transformation of operations models: a framework and a new research agenda. Prod Plan Control 28(11–12):929–944
Rosati E (2018) Why originality in copyright is not and should not be a meaningless requirement. J Intellectual Property Law Practice 13(8):597–598
Shadikhodjaev S (2021) Technological neutrality and regulation of digital trade: how far can we go? Eur J Int Law 32(4):1221–1247
Słok-Wódkowska M, Mazur J (2022) Secrecy by default: how regional trade agreements reshape protection of source code. J Int Econ Law 25(1):91–109
Trebilcock M, Trachtman J (2020) Advanced introduction to international trade law, 2nd edn. Edward Elgar Publishing, Cheltenham
Weber R (2015) Digital trade and E-commerce: challenges and opportunities of the Asia Pacific regionalism. Asian J WTO Int Health Law Policy 10(2):321–348
Weber R (2021) Global law in the face of Datafication and artificial intelligence. In: Peng S, Lin C, Streinz T (eds) Artificial intelligence and international economic law. Cambridge University Press, Cambridge, pp 54–69
World Economic Forum (2023) The fourth industrial revolution, by Klaus Schwab. https://perma.cc/W92U-9B4C
World Trade Organization (2000) Communication from the European Communities and their member states: electronic commerce work programme, https://docs.wto.org/dol2fe/Pages/SS/directdoc.aspx?filename=Q:/S/C/W183.pdf&Open=True
World Trade Organization (2018) World Trade Report 2018: the future of world trade: how digital technologies are transforming global commerce
Wunsch-Vincent S (2006a) The internet, cross-border trade in services, and the GATS: lessons from US–gambling. World Trade Rev 5(3):319–355
Wunsch-Vincent S (2006b) The WTO, the internet and trade in digital products: EC-US perspectives. Bloomsbury Publishing Plc, London
Wunsch-Vincent S, Hold A (2015) Towards coherent rules for digital trade. In: Burri M, Cottier T (eds) Trade governance in the digital age: world trade forum. Cambridge University Press, Cambridge, pp 179–221

Artificial Intelligence and International Arbitration

Yousra Mohamed Kamal

1 Introduction

While technology is evolving daily, some avoid it in the legal profession. Amidst this context, the COVID-19 pandemic has forced lawyers to incorporate technology into their regular tasks. The use of technology in the legal profession has opened the door to the utilization of AI in legal work. This section addresses the relationship between AI and alternative dispute resolution methods (ADR), especially international arbitration.

Online dispute resolution (ODR) is a more efficient settlement process that saves time, effort, and cost.[1] It uses information and communication technology. The process may be wholly online, or it could be hybrid.[2] As part of the new technology, AI is being used in ODR. The high-volume consumer disputes and mediation are two areas where AI is exceptionally adaptive. For instance, AI might assist parties in negotiations and find areas of overlap. ODR AI algorithms diagnose issues using vast amounts of past data and continuously learn from user input, helping big companies like eBay and Paypal to settle millions of complaints annually.[3]

Some countries also use AI to issue binding judgements and recommend outcomes to parties. For instance, In China's online courts, AI judges receive evidence, ask questions, set deadlines, and make rulings. Courts in Michigan, Ohio, California,

---

[1] Sadaphal (n.d.), p. 1. https://hcommons.org/deposits/objects/hc:57706/datastreams/CONTENT/content.

[2] *Ibid.*

[3] Dodokin et al. (n.d.).

Y. M. Kamal (✉)
LLM in International Commercial Law and Arbitration, Pepperdine School of Law, State Counsel, ESLA, Cairo, Egypt

A. Poorhashemi (ed.), *Artificial Intelligence and the Future of International Law*, SpringerBriefs in Law, https://doi.org/10.1007/978-3-031-73334-5_4

Wisconsin, and Utah have implemented algorithm-based ODR, primarily for low-conflict family court cases, small claims, traffic tickets, and outstanding warrant cases.[4]

2 How AI Works in ADR

AI can work in two different ways. First, AI can help facilitate legal work and enhance ADR efficiency by providing expert advice through document analysis, research, and standard drafting while identifying lies, assessing losses, predicting outcomes, and offering potential solutions.[5] The following are examples of AI tools that judges and lawyers may use as tools to facilitate their work:

(a) *Lex Machina* is an AI-powered legal analytics tool that can help lawyers with case analysis and litigation strategy. The tool uses algorithms to analyze data from past cases and provide insights into judges, lawyers, and outcomes. It can also provide information on damages awarded, case timelines, and legal precedents.[6]
(b) *DeepJudge* is an AI-powered knowledge search that helps legal professionals swiftly find and leverage insights from large document and knowledge management systems.[7]
(c) *Casetext*: an AI-powered legal research tool that can help with case law research and analysis. The tool uses natural language processing to quickly identify relevant cases and statutes and provide suggestions for legal arguments.[8]
(d) *ClauseBuilder*: The American Arbitration Association's ClauseBuilder can assist in developing clear and effective arbitration and mediation agreements.[9]

Second, some AI systems, like the ALATs discussed above, can work autonomously and even perform some of the functions of a lawyer, a mediator or an arbitrator. For instance, some AI tools can provide legal advice.[10] Further, in mediation, an AI algorithm can be used to search from its database for the most similar offer submitted by parties to its model solution, which encourages the parties to make logical solutions to be chosen by the algorithm.[11] The following are examples of this type of AI tools:

---

[4] Sadaphal (n.d.), p. 1. https://hcommons.org/deposits/objects/hc:57706/datastreams/CONTENT/content.

[5] Ibid., pp. 2–3.

[6] Lex Machina (n.d.).

[7] DeepJudge. (n.d.).

[8] Casetext. (n.d.).

[9] ClauseBuilder. (n.d.).

[10] Bennett et al. (2017).

[11] Sadaphal (n.d.), pp. 2–3. https://hcommons.org/deposits/objects/hc:57706/datastreams/CONTENT/content.

(a) ChatGPT as mediator: ChatGPT is an AI-based communication model trained on a large amount of data and has direct access to internet resources. It can understand, interpret, and respond to natural language that makes people feel like they are communicating with people. As communication is the heart of conflict resolution, especially in mediation, using ChatGPT as a mediator is seen by some as promising.[12]
(b) *Ross Intelligence*: This is the first artificial intelligent lawyer in the world, powered by IBM, recently accepted a position at the 900+ lawyer Baker & Hostetler law firm in New York, one of the biggest law firms in the world and the U.S. It can understand language, respond to inquiries, establish theories, and keep track of changes in the legal system.[13]
(c) *DoNotPay*: This tool is currently used in the U.S. and the U.K. It offers the chance to get parking fees reimbursed in around 30 s. Some prefer to consult DoNotPay rather than a human since the former operates through a chat window and uses a "*friendly, easy-to-understand language*."[14] DoNotPay now includes functions that help in demanding compensation for delayed flights and filing paperwork for assistance in government housing.[15]

3 How AI Can Be Used in Arbitration

In the following lines, we will address how AI can be used in arbitration and the concerns it raises.

3.1 AI and Choosing Arbitrators

Choosing arbitrators is a controversial process. There are options to choose a sole arbitrator or three arbitrators' tribunal, which is typically considered to be an essential benefit of arbitration. In the instance of a three-member tribunal, each party may recommend one arbitrator, and the two appointed arbitrators may appoint the chairperson.[16] Selecting arbitrators is crucial for the parties because there are few chances to challenge arbitral awards. Therefore, the parties in the dispute are keen to choose a knowledgeable tribunal to understand the merits and reach a fair decision.[17]

---

[12] More information about how ChatGPT can be used in mediation, pros and cons can be found in: Weisheit and Salger (2023, June 21).

[13] Yeşil (n.d.).

[14] Ibid.

[15] Bennett et al. (2017), p. 38.

[16] Stadwick (2013, June).

[17] Ibid.

AI can assist in choosing arbitrators with the required experience and also avoid choosing arbitrators that might have a conflict of interest according to the applicable rules, such as the International Bar Association (IBA) Guidelines on Conflicts of Interest in International Arbitration.[18]

In addition, AI can have a massive role in encouraging diversity and inclusion in the selection of arbitrators. Research shows a positive correlation between better team performance and greater diversity in arbitration. Applying these findings to tribunal formation may enhance efficiency by selecting arbitrators from diverse backgrounds. In the 2018 International Arbitration Survey, which was conducted by Queen Mary University of London and White & Case, 40% of respondents said that having a diverse panel of arbitrators would enhance the quality of the tribunal's decision-making, while 19% said that the question is irrelevant because diversity is valuable in and of itself.[19]

Nonetheless, the majority of arbitral panels are homogenous, predominantly consisting of old white males. According to the statistics of the ICCA's Report of the Cross-Institutional Task Force on Gender Diversity in Arbitral Appointments and Proceedings, arbitral institutions are leading in selecting women arbitrators and parties, but co-arbitrators still lag behind. In 2022, 27% of HKIAC appointments involved female arbitrators, while party and co-arbitrator appointments were low at 18.9% and 11.4%, respectively. In 2022, ICSID statistics showed that female arbitrators accounted for 24% of all ICSID appointments, with ICSID making 55%, parties making 39%, and co-arbitrators making 6%.[20]

Diversity should increase in terms of nationality, ethnicity, and age, in addition to having more women arbitrators.[21] Moreover, we must include new arbitrators because experienced arbitrators are often preferred over newcomers.[22]AI-based tools are not yet available for consumers to select arbitrators. We only have online databases that use data analytics to bridge the transparency gap in the arbitrator selection process.[23]

The following are examples of Arbitrators' databases:

(a) The AIQ (Arbitrator Intelligence Questionnaire) is a secure website run by Penn State University that conducts online polls. It permits the systematic

[18] "The IBA Guidelines on Conflicts of Interest focus on when an arbitrator should disclose potential conflicts, as well as when he or she should simply not accept appointment. For the most part, they do not specifically address the potential disqualification of an arbitrator. Nonetheless, the Guidelines, even though non-binding, have become quite influential in the face of increasing challenges to international arbitrators and awards on the basis of arbitrator conflicts. The Guidelines are frequently viewed by courts and arbitral institutions as providing relevant criteria for assessing the impartiality and independence of a challenged arbitrator." You can find more of this topic in: Moses (2017, November 23).

[19] Reynolds and Melendez (n.d.).

[20] Jain (2023, February 12).

[21] de Haas and Faienza (2022, November 8).

[22] Reynolds and Melendez (n.d.).

[23] Ibid.

gathering of input information about arbitrators' case management and decision-making that was previously only accessible through individualized one-on-one enquiries, typically over the phone, after each arbitration.[24] The AIQ produces reports that counsels and third-party funders can purchase. These reports are generated by compiling arbitrators' biographical data and their past decisions to increase objectivity in choosing arbitrators, which fosters diversity in choosing arbitrators.[25]

(b) GAR's Arbitrator Research Tool: It allows users to search by filters like language, nationality, gender, home city, experience, and specialization. Giving data regarding who worked with arbitrators recently, Arbitrator's procedural preferences, past awards, CVs, news, arbitrators' connections, information about new arbitrators, etc., help users get detailed data about experienced arbitrators at the same time, presenting the new arbitrators to users as well.[26]

(c) *Arbitrator Intelligence:* Arbitrator Intelligence is a nonprofit organization with academic ties. Through the publication of AI Reports, Arbitrator Intelligence aims to make essential data regarding arbitrators' prior decision-making more widely accessible to promote openness, accountability, and diversity in arbitrator selection.[27]

The logical next step in developing such technology is applying AI to augment the data analytics component of a typical database by sifting through a massive quantity of data to identify the "best" option for a specific scenario based on parties' expressed preferences.[28] This can be developed by requesting the user to enter their preferences, which could be listed based on the IBA Guidelines on Conflicts of Interest and the circumstances of each case. Then, the AI-based application can compile the available data to recommend the best options for the user.

Nonetheless, there are concerns that an AI system's automated selection of arbitrators may be somehow biased. For example, an AI may define a well-ranked arbiter as having good availability, making decisions quickly, and other characteristics. As a result, the algorithm might recognize that men should be appointed rather than pregnant women on temporary leave, for instance. Because of this bias, potential female arbitrators may receive a lower score and rank. Therefore, some say that AI should be used cautiously because its data input depends on human activity, which may "teach" the algorithm to act in a biased manner. And that the solution could be to prevent the use of data such as gender, age, ethnicity, etc., or at least handle them cautiously.[29]

The automated selection of arbitrators using AI algorithms is not something we can escape or avoid nowadays. Instead, it has great potential to overcome the

[24] Rogers (2018, February 27).

[25] Reynolds and Melendez (n.d.).

[26] GAR Arbitration Research Tool (ART). FAQ. (n.d.).

[27] Rogers (2018, February 27).

[28] Reynolds and Melendez (n.d.).

[29] Becker and Marques (n.d.).

concerns of arbitrators' selection, like lack of diversity and inclusion or the avoidance of newcomers. This could be clear when we focus on our role of ensuring that the database includes all arbitrators. The selection algorithm does not exclude any criteria unless guided by the user-submitted preferences or considering the applicable rules. Arbitration, in essence, is a consensual or optional dispute settlement process designed to be more efficient for the benefit of its parties. Therefore, the purpose of using new technology, including AI in its steps, should be to guarantee that the parties are well informed about all the available suitable options using a clear presentation. But the decision remains in their hands.

3.2 AI & Document Reviewing and Production

Document review and production are the most time-consuming and expensive parts of arbitration for both parties' counsels and arbitrators because the volume of the documents in international arbitration is enormous in most cases. In addition, the documents may need to be translated into the language of arbitration. Therefore, new technologies and AI applications for document review and production are essential for more efficient arbitration.

The IBA has published a list of some of the potential technology resources to be used for these purposes.[30] The list was divided into three categories as follows:

(a) DOCUMENT REVIEW PLATFORMS: allow uploading, reviewing, and coding of large volumes of data from a single platform, reducing electronic data volume through culling tools like deduplication and email threading. They also convert image files, index documents, and identify media files for critical document identification. Ex: Relativity and Ringtail (Nuix Discover).
(b) SOFTWARE/AI APPLICATIONS FOR DOCUMENT REVIEW: It can assist in the collection and review of documents in unstructured data formats, such as chats, MMS, and SMS messages. It can also help visualize data like email trends and social network visualizations. Auto-redaction software tools can reduce the time needed for linear review of documents containing privileged and sensitive information. These tools can automatically find and redact sensitive information. Technology-assisted review (TAR), continuous active learning, and predictive coding can help categorize and code large amounts of documents in a shorter time. Continuous active learning models identify responsive documents and apply them to the remaining documents, adjusting coding accordingly. Ex: Brainspace, KLDiscovery, NexLP, Sentio Software, and Veritone.

[30] Technology resources for arbitration practitioners - Document collection, review, and production. (n.d.).

(c) SPECIALISED VENDORS: Numerous vendors offer electronic data collection, processing, hosting, document review, and production services: Consilio, Epiq, KLDiscovery, Law In Order, and XDD (Xact Data Discovery).

As some practitioners suggest, AI has massive potential in arranging documents, reducing their volume, excluding duplicated documents, and translating documents of Arbitration. However, some documents need a second human eye to ensure the AI functions accurately. Significantly, the handwritten documents and government documents issued in some countries are written in languages other than English. In addition, regarding the counsel's work, deciding which documents are relevant and in favour of the party cannot be managed through AI applications only because AI power and accuracy come from the amount of data in its database. This fact is problematic in arbitration due to the lack of information available due to the confidentiality of the proceedings. Almost always, only the parties to the arbitration have their cases' documents and awards.[31]

Similarly, regarding the arbitrators' work, AI applications will not be able to give an accurate outcome or predict the outcome of each case. AI technology may not be ready for the potential of predictive technology in arbitration due to privacy and confidentiality concerns. Besides, AI has limited ability to handle complex and unpredictable elements of arbitration, such as reasoning and recognition, and there are also concerns regarding impartiality. While AI may reduce human error, bias, and distraction, parties may be unready to trust a virtual arbitrator whose thought process is shrouded in a "black box" while they cannot ensure that programmer biases are not incorporated into the algorithm.[32]

3.3 *Transparency and Impartiality in AI Arbitration*

Procedurally, there is no guarantee that the AI arbitrator's decision will be bias-free because machine learning-based programs set the guidelines for AI arbitrators with no sufficient transparency. Besides, it is challenging for AI system designers to identify the mistakes or the algorithms that lead to those mistakes. Moreover, this technological knowledge is beyond the lawyers' expertise. For these reasons, setting aside an arbitral award on the grounds of impartiality is more challenging in the case of AI arbitration.[33]

Further, following the applicable arbitration rules, the arbitrator must disclose any circumstances that could question the arbitrator's impartiality. If the arbitrator is proven to have acted in a biased manner, they will be removed from the case without the need to prove such bias in the final award. On the contrary, in the case of the AI arbitrator, the bias can be identified in the algorithm only after reviewing

[31] IA vs. AI: Genuine arbitration in the time of artificial intelligence. (n.d.).

[32] Dodokin et al. (n.d.).

[33] *Implementation of artificial intelligence in arbitration*. (2021, December 1).

the use or result of such a biased algorithm in the final award. At the same time, the disclosure of algorithms at the outset of the arbitration will not prevent the bias effect of the disclosed algorithm. This issue represents a legal concern in the case of AI Arbitrators.[34] In other words, the use of an AI system causes a "black box" problem, wherein humans, even those who designed the AI system, cannot understand how variables are being combined to make automated predictions. Thus, even assuming that AI can make accurate predictions, it operates in a manner that humans cannot fully understand. This fact creates discomfort over the implementation and use of AI in Arbitration.[35]

3.4 *Due Process in AI Arbitration*

Arbitration requires minimum procedural safeguards to maintain confidence in its integrity, including valid delegation of jurisdictional powers, arbitrators, and enforcement of awards.[36] Arbitration involves facts, laws, and applying rules to a case. The application of laws to facts is considered intelligence. AI arbitrators are trying to do this task. However, establishing facts is challenging due to subjective opinions and legal ramifications.

Similarly, the question of law in AI arbitration is also challenging because it interplays with the facts of the case, especially when the legal question is not binary with a yes/no answer and cannot be separated from questioning the fact the law defines as legally relevant. Hence, applying the law to facts remains an essential concern for AI arbitration because AI models predict case outcomes relying on judicial decisions without questioning any partiality or neutrality of the judges or the way they decide favourable or unfavourable facts in judgments.[37] Regarding examining witnesses, scholars suggest that AI arbitrators can perform witness examinations with the help of other AI models. For example, it could use an AI model to check if the witness is lying and incorporate the finding into the case's outcome. However, human ability surpasses machine learning, particularly in commonsense knowledge and reasoning, which raises concerns regarding the legitimacy of AI arbitration.[38]

Moreover, it is difficult for robots to determine disputes that turn on factual judgment. For example, which of the two witnesses the robot will believe and why? Noting that a failure to give sufficient weight to the factual details of a case might constitute a breach of the right to be heard.[39] AI arbitrators face challenges in

---

[34] Ibid.

[35] Seet et al.. (2023, May 25).

[36] Kasap (2021, June 9), p. 32. https://ssrn.com/abstract=3863136.

[37] Ibid., p. 38.

[38] Ibid., pp. 39–40.

[39] Maxwell (2019, January 17).

providing proper reasoning for outcomes, which is crucial for parties to accept or challenge awards. Besides, current studies show that AI algorithms can predict court decisions but cannot provide conventional reasons. All the more, human arbitrators can create innovative doctrines, unlike AI arbitrators, who cannot step outside the box to respond to international commerce demands or have the flexibility to develop rules and standards of the Lex Mercatoria.[40] The above-addressed reasons may affect the sustainability of the arbitration process itself as a favourable resort to settle commercial disputes.

3.5 *AI Arbitration and Hearing*

With regard to procedural meetings, As stipulated in most arbitration rules, during case management conferences or hearings and subject to approval by the arbitral tribunal, parties set arbitration timelines and deadlines in a procedural timetable.[41] An AI arbitrator has an excellent potential to administer the procedural meeting through an algorithm, asking the parties specific questions with a specific hierarchy and ensuring equal time allocation for both parties. It's an effective way to save time and cost. Such an AI model can be used in regular arbitration with an arbitral tribunal. In this instance, the arbitral tribunal will also be asked relevant questions to approve the procedural timetable of the arbitration pursuant to the applicable rules. It could be a good application of gamification[42]in AI arbitration to streamline the process.

Regarding the other hearings, AI arbitrators can conduct hearings on various aspects of a case, including jurisdiction, liability, and damages.[43] These hearings can be transcribed, with no room for questions related to merits or pleadings. The proceedings may be conducted solely on documents and other materials, eliminating the need for oral hearings, which may not be favourable to arbitration practitioners.

[40] Ibid., pp. 40–43.

[41] Procedural timetable under the ICC rules. (n.d.).

[42] Gamification is the process of adding game elements to concepts that don't have a gaming context. The main reason why gamification is so valuable is that it boosts user engagement. It makes tasks that people usually consider challenging more fun and, therefore, easier. (n.d.).

[43] Gamification and AI – The future is now. Oral hearing - UNCITRAL arbitration. (n.d.). https://icsid.worldbank.org/procedures/arbitration/uncitral/oral-hearing.

3.6 Can AI Arbitrators Be Used in Institutional Arbitration?

Most of the institutional arbitration rules are silent regarding AI. The most they permit are virtual hearings and case management conferences. Therefore, institutional arbitration can use AI arbitrators, especially if the rules do not define an arbitrator as a human.[44] However, some scholars argue that even though some institutional arbitration rules, like the ICC International Court of Arbitration Rules of 2020 in Article 13 thereof, do not require a human to render an arbitral award, the use of machine arbitrators may be challenging due to legal, ethical, and procedural issues, as well as to be valid in relevant jurisdictions for the enforcement purposes.[45] While there has yet to be an arbitration case where an AI has served as an arbitrator to date, there are already some court cases where AI tools performed some aspects of judicial decision-making. AI has been used in bail hearings in the U.S. to predict the risk of absconding.[46] Further, AI has been used in determining the appropriate sentences in some criminal cases. One of the most notable examples of such cases is the infamous *Loomis v. Wisconsin*.[47] In said case, the judge used a risk assessment software called COMPAS (Correctional Offender Management Profiling for Alternative Sanctions) in determining the appropriate sentence to be imposed upon Eric Loomis, who pled guilty to Attempting to Flee or Elude a Traffic Officer and to Operating a Motor Vehicle without Owner's consent. Since COMPAS classified Loomis as high-risk of re-offending, he was sentenced to 6 years in prison. Loomis challenged the court's reliance on COMPAS, arguing that it violated his due process rights because the proprietary nature of the software prevented him from assailing the scientific validity of the risk assessment and that it took his gender and race into account when formulating the assessment. However, Loomis' challenge was unsuccessful as the U.S. Supreme Court denied his petition for *certiorari*, thereby refusing to reverse the Wisconsin Supreme Court's finding that no due process right was violated.

3.7 Cyber Security and AI Arbitration

The increasing digitalization and remote proceedings necessitate cybersecurity investments to protect arbitration frameworks and maintain the credibility of this method, especially since confidentiality is a vital issue in arbitration.[48] ICCA-NYC

---

44 Habib (n.d.).

45 Amro (2021), pp. 1–8. http://www.abacademies.org/articles/the-use-of-a-machine-arbitrator-as-an-application-of-artificial-intelligence-in-making-arbitral-awards-11993.html.

46 Maxwell (2019, January 17).

47 Loomis v. Wisconsin, U.S. Supreme Court, Case No. 16-6387 (2017).

48 Furlan (2021, September).

Bar-CPR Protocol on Cybersecurity in International Arbitration[49] recommends raising information regarding security issues from the start of proceedings. Parties, arbitrators, and representatives must study factors like data to be processed, risk analysis, existing security practices, and consequences of breaches. It is crucial to balance financial and technical resources to prevent onerous measures that might reduce the efficiency of the arbitration process.

Likewise, prior consultation with the arbitral institution is essential to ensure consistency and adequacy. Also, all the stockholders should be educated about the security measures, including independent contractors and third parties, because a successful attack can impact everyone involved, causing financial losses, reputational damage, and information authenticity risks.[50] The Cybersecurity Protocol emphasizes the crucial role of tribunals in cybersecurity measures, especially when parties have differing opinions or legal obligations. The tribunal should harmonize obligations, discuss security measures, and create a digital protection framework. However, it may involve interference in decisions, protecting third-party interests, maintaining arbitrators' capabilities, and maintaining proceedings' legitimacy. The tribunal may also impose sanctions in case of information security incidents, but this can be limited by law.

Moreover, data protection laws, such as the GDPR, apply to arbitration. In this context, Parties to arbitration are charged with specific obligations; parties and arbitrators are considered data controllers; administering institutions and third parties serve as data processors. Accordingly, the arbitral tribunal is responsible for complying with data protection, recording measures, and issuing directions. The GDPR also requires the tribunal to provide parties with information about their rights.[51]

The arbitral tribunal's proactive role in cybersecurity and its role as data controller are essential concerns that should be addressed in the case of AI arbitration and how these roles could be done through algorithms.

[49] The Cybersecurity Protocol for International Arbitration, released in 2019 and updated in 2022, aims to establish reasonable information-security measures for individual arbitration matters and raise awareness about international arbitrations. *The Cybersecurity Protocol for International Arbitration*. (2019, updated 2022). http://documents.nycbar.org/files/ICCA-NYC-Bar-CPR-Cybersecurity-Protocol-for-International-Arbitration-Electronic-Version.pdf.

[50] Furlan, J. G. (n.d.). *Cybersecurity on international arbitration and the role of the arbitral tribunal*. http://www.vyablog.com/2021/09/cybersecurity-on-international.html.

[51] Ibid.

3.8 *What's Next: Blockchain Arbitration and AI Arbitration in Metaverse*

Blockchain[52] arbitration has been developed as the dispute resolution mechanism of choice for disputes arising from smart contracts, which are entirely written in code and automatically execute or enforce obligations. For instance, in a simple contract to sell an item, the contract is coded to automatically transfer the ownership to the buyer once the payment is made. Blockchain arbitration is required to settle complex contracts, which may include misunderstandings in the transaction. Examples of models of blockchain arbitration are CodeLegit and Kleros.[53] However, there are several fundamental issues regarding blockchain arbitration that prevent it from replacing regular arbitration, especially in the context of international arbitration. The contract entirely written in code may not be valid in some national laws, and the coded arbitral clause may not fulfill the requirement under the New York Convention for the arbitral clause to be in writing. Lastly, some models of blockchain arbitration, like Kleros, are not developed to hear any arguments from the disputing parties, which will be a barrier for enforcing awards according to the New York Convention for not allowing the party to present its case.[54] Here is a glimpse of the future, as some predicted that by 2030, a significant fraction of individuals will participate in the Metaverse,[55] which is defined as "*the next evolution in social connection and the successor to the mobile internet.*"[56]

The metaverse allows ownership of various digital assets, including wearables, collectibles, and virtual land.[57] As the Metaverse's growth signifies mass adoption of virtual assets, it will enable autonomous arbitration, "without state interference" because the use of blockchain arbitration will enable the immediate award enforcement as shown below: Smart contracts, the base of the blockchain arbitration, enable digitally executable remedies, such as monetary compensation awards. Money can be digitally represented and transferred to the winning party from an account linked to the contract. But the scope of autonomous arbitration in the metaverse will be limited by the amount of screw the parties have transferred before the arbitration.

[52] Blockchain is a method of recording information that makes it impossible or difficult for the system to be changed, hacked, or manipulated. A blockchain is a distributed ledger that duplicates and distributes transactions across the network of computers participating in the blockchain. Blockchain technology is a structure that stores transactional records, also known as the block, of the public in several databases, known as the "chain," in a network connected through peer-to-peer nodes. Typically, this storage is referred to as a 'digital ledger. Every transaction in this ledger is authorized by the digital signature of the owner, which authenticates the transaction and safeguards it from tampering. Hence, the information the digital ledger contains is highly secure." More of this topic available at: Ravikiran (2023, July 21).

[53] Yeoh (2018, March 29).

[54] Ibid.

[55] Mac Ghlionn and Hamilton (2022, January 8).

[56] T*he metaverse: What is it?* (n.d.).

[57] Vijayan (2022, March 11).

And if an award requires a higher sum than available in escrow or linked accounts, parties may seek court intervention. However, as suggested by some scholars, blockchain arbitration can address this issue by controlling parties' assets through digital representation in the Metaverse, like non-fungible tokens (NFTs) linked to smart contracts.[58]

AI can be used in blockchain arbitration to resolve disputes as an algorithm within the smart contract that would resolve disputes by finding its reasoning based on similar situations in other blockchains, especially since all information in a public blockchain is accessible to users.[59]

4 Conclusion

After we addressed the opportunities and challenges facing AI and international arbitration in the previous pages, we can say that using AI in arbitration is inevitable, but the scope of usage and how far it can extend is the core of the discussion. As shown above, there are many concerns about using AI in international arbitration, including but not limited to algorithms' ability to conduct tasks, confidentiality, impartiality, due process requirements, enforcement, and validity in national jurisdictions.

In addition, many questions need to be answered: can AI be used in investment arbitration? Can AI entirely replace lawyers in international arbitration? Can avatars replace arbitrators in international arbitration? Can AI maintain the sustainability of international arbitration as a method to settle disputes? Is there a difference between consumer and complex arbitration in using AI? These questions must be answered at all levels: scholars, practitioners, legislators, etc. There are many challenges to adopting AI in international arbitration. Still, the road of technology is tailored to human needs and at some point, the law streamlines the road to use new technologies. However, AI is far from replacing humans in the legal field because human capabilities surpass machine learning in this context. We may need thousands of algorithms to replace humans in the dispute settlement process. Assuming we have these dream AI models, the door will be opened for other problems, including confidentiality and security, which will decrease the process's integrity and efficiency. The International Labour Organization found in its latest report published in August 2023 that "*AI tools likely to complement jobs not to destroy them*".[60]

Throughout history, humanity has used technology to solve social and economic problems. International law in this regard should be evidence-based and limit negative impacts on human rights and the rule of law. The current economic development situation has accelerated the adoption of various technologies in the law

[58] Ibid.

[59] Rodsphon (n.d.).

[60] Gmyrek et al. (2023, August 21).

industries. The arbitration community, whose goals include efficient and cost-effective dispute resolution, should be open to adopting any technology that achieves these goals, including AI. Undoubtedly, there are unanswered questions regarding integrating AI, meeting all parties' needs and gaining the trust of arbitration users. In this perspective, the technology could be welcomed in certain areas, such as the non-consensual selection of an arbitrator, assessing the risks or likelihood of an event occurring, and recognizing trends in documents and other fact-finding processes.

International cooperation is crucial to regulate AI worldwide. Improving interactions between different levels and actors at national and international levels is crucial to participating in regulatory processes appropriate for AI regulations.

While a genuinely binding international treaty would be more appropriate, it must first be successfully negotiated and a sufficient number of ratifications obtained from countries committed to effective national implementation through legal framework changes. Within the Council of Europe framework, negotiations should begin in May 2022 to adopt a binding text on artificial intelligence. Such effort could be developed at the global level.

All these issues seem to lead us towards the emergence of "artificial intelligence law" in the future.

References

Amro I (2021) The use of a machine arbitrator as an application of artificial intelligence in making arbitral awards. J Legal Ethical Regul Iss 24(S4):1–8. http://www.abacademies.org/articles/the-use-of-a-machine-arbitrator-as-an-application-of-artificial-intelligence-in-making-arbitral-awards-11993.html

Becker D, Marques RD (n.d.) Why the use of technology in arbitrators' selection process - Although fostered - must still be handled carefully. https://cbar.org.br/site/why-the-use-of-technology-in-arbitrators-selection-process-although-fostered-must-still-be-handled-carefully/

Bennett J, Miller T, Webb J, Bosua R, Lodders A, Chamberlain S (2017) Current state of automated legal advice tools. Networked Society Institute Working Paper. https://doi.org/10.13140/RG.2.2.17230.51520

Casetext (n.d.). https://casetext.com/

ClauseBuilder (n.d.). https://clausebuilder.org/

de Haas E, Faienza V (2022, November 8) Arbitration's age of enlightenment? A look back at ICCA Edinburgh 2022. https://arbitrationblog.kluwerarbitration.com/2022/11/08/arbitrations-age-of-enlightenment-a-look-back-at-icca-edinburgh-2022/

DeepJudge (n.d.) Product. https://deepjudge.ai/product

Dodokin R, McEachern S, Honywill L (n.d.) Artificial intelligence and arbitration: a perfect fit? https://adric.ca/artificial-intelligence-and-arbitration-a-perfect-fit/#ftn2

Furlan JG (2021, September) Cybersecurity on international arbitration and the role of the arbitral tribunal. http://www.vyablog.com/2021/09/cybersecurity-on-international.html

Gamification and AI – The future is now. Oral hearing - UNCITRAL arbitration (n.d.). https://icsid.worldbank.org/procedures/arbitration/uncitral/oral-hearing

Gamification is the process of adding game elements to concepts that don't have a gaming context. The main reason why gamification is so valuable is that it boosts user engagement. It makes

tasks that people usually consider challenging more fun and, therefore, easier (n.d.). https://www.etrellium.com/ai/where-do-gamification-and-ai-converge/
GAR Arbitration Research Tool (ART). FAQ (n.d.). https://globalarbitrationreview.com/tools/arbitrator-research-tool/faq
Gmyrek P, Berg J, Bescond D (2023, August 21) Generative AI and jobs: A global analysis of potential effects on job quantity and quality. https://www.ilo.org/static/english/intserv/working-papers/wp096/index.html
Habib S (n.d.) The use of artificial intelligence in arbitration in Africa—Inevitable or unachievable? https://www.ibanet.org/article/E62B06F6-7772-458A-A6E7-1474DB7136B5
IA vs. AI: Genuine arbitration in the time of artificial intelligence (n.d.). https://www.sciencespo.fr/ecole-de-droit/fr/actualites/ia-vs-ai-genuine-arbitration-time-artificial-intelligence.html
Implementation of artificial intelligence in arbitration (2021, December 1) Master's thesis, University of Oslo, Faculty of Law. Supervised by S. F. Schwemer. https://www.duo.uio.no/bitstream/handle/10852/92206/ICTLTHESIS%2D%2D-Master-Thesis.pdf?sequence=1
Jain S (2023, February 12) 2022 year in review: diversity in the mainstream. https://arbitrationblog.kluwerarbitration.com/2023/02/12/2022-year-in-review-diversity-in-the-mainstream/
Kasap GH (2021) Can artificial intelligence ('AI') replace human arbitrators? Technological concerns and legal implications. J Dispute Resol 2021(2):32. https://ssrn.com/abstract=3863136
Lex Machina (n.d.). https://lexmachina.com/
Loomis v. Wisconsin, U.S. Supreme Court, Case No. 16-6387 (2017)
MacGhlionn J, Hamilton B (2022, January 8) Metaverse clothing, travel, plastic surgery: Experts predict life in 2030. https://nypost.com/2022/01/08/experts-predict-living-in-the-metaverse-by-2030/#
Maxwell K (2019, January 17) Summoning the demon: Robot arbitrators: Arbitration and artificial intelligence. http://arbitrationblog.practicallaw.com/summoning-the-demon-robot-arbitrators-arbitration-and-artificial-intelligence/
Moses M (2017, November 23) The role of the IBA Guidelines on conflicts of interest in arbitrator challenges. https://arbitrationblog.kluwerarbitration.com/2017/11/23/role-iba-guidelines-conflicts-interest-arbitrator-challenges/
Procedural timetable under the ICC rules (n.d.). https://www.acerislaw.com/procedural-timetable-under-the-icc-rules/
Ravikiran AS (2023, July 21) What is blockchain technology? How does blockchain work? https://www.simplilearn.com/tutorials/blockchain-tutorial/blockchain-technology
Reynolds A, Melendez P (n.d.) AI arbitrator selection tools and diversity on arbitral panels. https://www.ibanet.org/article/97cb79fa-39e9-48c1-8cb0-45569e2e62af
Rodsphon J (n.d.) Blockchain technology & AI arbitration: What may the future hold? https://www.ipg-online.org/data/cms_uploads/module_partner/publications/article%20%20arbitration%20and%20AI-blockchain.pdf
Rogers CA (2018, February 27) Arbitrator intelligence: The basics. https://arbitrationblog.kluwerarbitration.com/2018/02/27/ai-3/
Sadaphal Y (n.d.) AI in ADR: An analysis. Indian J Law Legal Res 5(3):1–3. https://hcommons.org/deposits/objects/hc:57706/datastreams/CONTENT/content
Seet A, Lim B, Tasende I (2023, May 25) Arbitration tech toolbox: looking beyond the black box of AI in disputes over AI's use. https://arbitrationblog.kluwerarbitration.com/2023/05/25/arbitration-tech-toolbox-looking-beyond-the-black-box-of-ai-in-disputes-over-ais-use/
Stadwick J (2013, June) Four factors to consider when selecting an arbitrator. https://www.tamimi.com/law-update-articles/four-factors-to-consider-when-selecting-an-arbitrator/
Technology resources for arbitration practitioners - Document collection, review, and production (n.d.). https://www.ibanet.org/technology-resources-for-arbitration-documents
The Cybersecurity Protocol for International Arbitration (2022). http://documents.nycbar.org/files/ICCA-NYC-Bar-CPR-Cybersecurity-Protocol-for-International-Arbitration-Electronic-Version.pdf
The metaverse: What is it? (n.d.). https://www.searchenginejournal.com/metaverse/484803/#close

Vijayan S (2022, March 11) Autonomous arbitration in the era of the metaverse. https://arbitrationblog.kluwerarbitration.com/2022/03/11/autonomous-arbitration-in-the-era-of-the-metaverse/
Weisheit S, Salger C (2023, June 21) Artificial intelligence (AI) in mediation—ChatGPT as mediator 4.0. https://mediate.com/artificial-intelligence-ai-in-mediation-chatgpt-as-mediator-4-0/
Yeoh D (2018, March 29) Is online dispute resolution the future of alternative dispute resolution? https://arbitrationblog.kluwerarbitration.com/2018/03/29/online-dispute-resolution-future-alternative-dispute-resolution/
Yeşil C (n.d.) Robot judges & judicial actors of artificial intelligence. http://www.ilsaedergi.com/en/robot-judges-judicial-actors-of-artificial-intelligence/

General Conclusion

Abbas Poorhashemi

This book examines the relationship between artificial intelligence (AI) and international law, from human rights and criminal law to trade and arbitration perspectives. The massive development of artificial intelligence in many different professionals, services, and industries shows that it is essential for our current and future generations. Artificial intelligence is a technology that is increasingly integrating into people's lives. Although AI has numerous functions and assists in many parts, there are concerns about its potentially disruptive effects on some sectors, including international law. This evolution requires new regulations and standards to utilize this technology nationally and internationally. This book reviews some potential aspects of international law arising from the emergence of AI and discusses AI's implications on some parts of international law. This book shows that while AI could improve human life in many ways, it could raise concerns about the primacy of the rule of law, human rights, criminal law, and even international trade and arbitration. This research recommends that international organizations, states, and the private sector cooperate to ensure that human rights and the rule of law are respected when utilizing AI at national and international levels.

The increased utilization of artificial intelligence has created numerous global challenges and opportunities facing international law. From human rights violations to facilitating health diagnostics, from employment threats to enabling human interactions through social media are only some examples of the application of this new technology in our modern society. Moreover, the challenges related to AI require a response from international law.

International law faces the diversity of the AI standards, the plurality of its utilisations and the absence of a universal definition of AI and its regulation. The current international legal framework for AI is insufficient. The difficulty lies in that

A. Poorhashemi (✉)
Canadian Institute for International Law Expertise (CIFILE), Toronto, ON, Canada
e-mail: info@cifile.org

A. Poorhashemi (ed.), *Artificial Intelligence and the Future of International Law*, SpringerBriefs in Law, https://doi.org/10.1007/978-3-031-73334-5_5

regulating AI requires recourse to several branches of law and types of rules that fall under national and international law.

The development of Artificial intelligence in the contemporary world requires a response to international law. Establishing and implementing international regulations to deal with these new technologies is crucial for the future development of international law.

In response to the challenges facing the utilization of AI, some States and international organizations are looking for a legal framework to minimize the risks associated with AI. The European Commission was the first to publish in April 2021 a proposal for a regulation on a legal framework for artificial intelligence, which has not yet been adopted.[1] At the national level, In June 2022, Canada also published a proposed law on artificial intelligence and data (Bill C-27).[2] However, the regulations and legislation are insufficient to create a framework and legal status of AI at national and international levels.

This research proposed that the international community should create a global mechanism dealing with artificial intelligence. The global institution may advise and assist states and international organizations in establishing and implementing international regulations.

[1] EU AI Act: first regulation on artificial intelligence. The use of artificial intelligence in the EU will be regulated by the AI Act, the world's first comprehensive AI law. Published: 08-06-2023. For more see: https://www.europarl.europa.eu/topics/en/article/20230601STO93804/eu-ai-act-first-regulation-on-artificial-intelligence#:~:text=In%20April%202021%2C%20the%20European,mean%20more%20or%20less%20regulation.

[2] Bill C-27, An Act to enact the Consumer Privacy Protection Act, the Personal Information and Data Protection Tribunal Act and the Artificial Intelligence and Data Act and to make consequential and related amendments to other Acts, is also known as the Digital Charter Implementation Act, 2022. The Consumer Privacy Protection Act is Part 1 of the Digital Charter Implementation Act, 2022. The Consumer Privacy Protection Act would repeal parts of the Personal Information Protection and Electronic Documents Act and replace them with a new legislative regime governing the collection, use, and disclosure of personal information for commercial activity in Canada. This would maintain, modernize, and extend existing rules and impose new rules on private sector organizations for the protection of personal information. The Consumer Privacy Protection Act would also continue and enhance the role of the Privacy Commissioner in overseeing organizations' compliance with these measures. Provisions of the Personal Information Protection and Electronic Documents Act addressing electronic alternatives to paper records would be retained under the new title of the Electronic Documents Act. Part 2 of the Digital Charter Implementation Act, 2022 contains the Personal Information and Data Protection Tribunal Act. It would create a new administrative tribunal to hear appeals of orders issued by the Privacy Commissioner and apply a new administrative monetary penalty regime created under the Consumer Privacy Protection Act. Part 3 of the Digital Charter Implementation Act, 2022, the Artificial Intelligence and Data Act, sets out new measures to regulate international and interprovincial trade and commerce in artificial intelligence systems. It would establish common requirements for the design, development, and use of artificial intelligence systems, including measures to mitigate risks of harm and biased output. It would also prohibit specific practices with data and artificial intelligence systems that may result in serious harm to individuals or their interests. For more see: https://www.justice.gc.ca/eng/csj-sjc/pl/charter-charte/c27_1.html#:~:text=on%20the%20Bill.Overview,Digital%20Charter%20Implementation%20Act%2C%202022.

Most AI initiatives developed globally in recent years have primarily occurred without regulatory oversight. Except for ethical guidelines, lawmakers worldwide have yet to design national laws that specifically regulate the use of AI. National legislation may mitigate the risk of AI at the national level.

It is important to note that the balance between encouraging the development of new technologies and protecting human rights is crucial for regulating and implementing laws at the national and international levels.

For future research regarding artificial intelligence and international law, it is vital to consider States and international organizations have voluntary commitment based on ethical principles and technical standards to protect human rights, the evolution of Soft law and encouragement of national legislation and finally, normative development by accepting and implementing international treaties and conventions to regulate the use of AI.

Made in the USA
Monee, IL
14 September 2026

63090694R00044